men's gymnastics

horizontal bar

Consultant

Dr. Irvin Faria
Sacramento State College
Sacramento, California

published by:

The Athletic Institute

Merchandise Mart, Chicago

*A not-for-profit organization
devoted to the advancement of
athletics, physical education
and recreation.*

1

Library of Congress
Catalog Card Number 79-109498

"Sports Techniques" Series
SBN 87670-055-5

Published by The Athletic Institute
Chicago, Illinois 60654

Foreword

The SPORTS TECHNIQUES SERIES is but one item in a comprehensive list of sports instructional aids which are made available by The Athletic Institute. This book is part of a master plan which seeks to make the benefits of athletics, physical education and recreation available to everyone.

The Athletic Institute is a not-for-profit organization devoted to the advancement of athletics, physical education and recreation. The Institute believes that participation in athletics and recreation has benefits of inestimable value to the individual and to the community.

The nature and scope of the many Institute programs are determined by a *Professional Advisory Committee,* whose members are noted for their outstanding knowledge, experience and ability in the fields of athletics, physical education and recreation.

The Institute believes that through this book the reader will become a better performer, skilled in the fundamentals of this fine event. Knowledge and the practice necessary to mold knowledge into playing ability are the keys to real enjoyment in playing any game or sport.

Gymnastics aids in the development of motor skills, flexibility, agility and endurance as well as providing enjoyable recreation.

The Athletic Institute

Introduction

Of the apparatus events, the horizontal bar is the most basic. Movements on the horizontal bar require basic swing technique which forms the groundwork for the other apparatus events. As with the other events, the basic laws of mechanics must be followed if excellence in swing technique is to be developed.

Two basic types of movements set the pattern for all horizontal bar skills. These movements are termed long and short swings. The long swing movements and combinations are performed at arm's length from the bar while the body is fully extended. Short swing skills and combinations are executed with the arms extended or bent while the body approaches but does not contact the bar.

Characteristic of basic and advanced work on the horizontal bar are hand changes. By means of hand changes and various hand grip positions, the gymnast is able to execute turns and rotations through the body's longitudinal and transverse axes. A routine should show a combination of flowing swings without a halt and without an intermediate or empty swing. Essentially movements which combine to form a routine should vary in type, including long and short circles performed in the front and back swings and supports. The structure of a fundamental exercise shows a balance between long circles, short circles and vaults.

Irvin Faria

Table of Contents

Table of Contents (Continued)

grasp

Though grasps differ for each hand position, all are taken with the thumb wrapped around the bar in an opposing direction to the fingers. It is essential that all grasps be applied with the whole hand, not just the fingers.

Grips

Overgrasp

The overgrasp (regular grip) grip is the most fundamental grip. It is used for swinging forward, under the bar or on top.

Undergrasp

The undergrasp grip is used for swinging in the opposite direction to that of the overgrasp. Most grips used are such that pressure is exerted against the fingers.

Mixed or Combined Grasp

One hand is in the undergrasp; the other hand is in the overgrasp. This basic grasp is used when vaulting and turning about the body's longitudinal axis.

Cross Grasp (Undergrasp)

This mixed grasp is somewhat specialized for moving into and out of turns about the body's longitudinal axis.

Cross Grasp (Overgrasp)

This grasp is primarily applied when turning about a longitudinal axis from long circles.

Rotated Grasp

This advanced grasp is used for advanced movements with the arms in inward rotation.

basic swings

Simple Swing

The learning of proper swing technique is essential prior to attempting even the most elementary movements on the horizontal bar. Movements are executed by means of free swing while strength is used only for body alignment. A good swing utilizes the hands as the fulcrum. If this principle is not followed, an inelegant routine is the end result.

From an erect stand facing the bar, jump to a hang on the bar in an overgrasp. The hand placement should be about a shoulder's-width apart and the thumb and fingers on opposite sides of the bar. Pull to a three-quarter, chin-up position while piking slightly at the hips and raising the legs about waist high. Simultaneously, lean back onto the shoulders and extend from the hips, thrusting the leg upward and outward. Continue to extend throughout the entire body.

As the body reaches its full extension, relax and swing free from the hands. At the end of the backward swing, slip the hands up over the bar to regain a firm grasp for the forward swing. Gradually increase the swing by swinging the legs forward from the hips as the body passes under the bar. Follow the leg lift with a forward and upward thrust through the hips and legs.

On the back swing, keep the shoulders forward and see that the legs swing back first. The hip movement under the bar is a scooping action followed by a body extension. The arms must remain straight while pressing the body away from the bar.

1. **ALWAYS EXTEND THROUGH SHOULDERS.**

2. **MAINTAIN GOOD FORM, LEGS STRAIGHT AND TOGETHER WITH TOES POINTED.**

3. **USE ENTIRE BODY FOR SWING ACTION.**

4. **MASTER SCOOP WITH LEGS, AND ALWAYS FOLLOW WITH GOOD HIP EXTENSION.**

Swinging Half Turns

Once the simple swing is mastered, attempt a half turn on the front swing. The turn should be smooth and the hand change, confident. Begin with a small swing. Move the hands together noting that the hands are in an overgrasp grip at the back swing.

Swing forward, scooping with the hips and legs. As in a normal swing, extend through the hips and shoulders when the upward movement begins. At this moment, move the head and shoulders to the left.

Release the right hand and carry it around under the bar as the shoulder turns. Regrasp the bar in an overgrasp on the far side of the left hand. The hands are now in a mixed grasp.

1. **KEEP LEGS SQUEEZED TOGETHER AT ALL TIMES.**

2. PRESS AWAY FROM BAR WITH PIVOT ARM DURING TURN.

3. EXTEND THROUGH SHOULDERS AND HIPS AS THE TURN IS INITIATED.

4. HAVE A FIRM OVERGRASP WITH PIVOT HAND.

5. JUST PRIOR TO THE TURN, WATCH TOES RISE.

6. TURN HEAD UNDER PIVOT ARM.

Cast Backward to Long Underswing

From a front support, with the hands in an overgrasp, bend the arms allowing the stomach to touch the bar. Hold the shoulders in front of the hands while the legs move slightly forward under the bar to place the body in a slight jackknife position.

Keep the shoulders forward of the hands and whip the legs backward and upward while pushing down on the bar. At this moment thrust away from the bar straightening the arms. The seat leads the legs, followed by an extension through the hips. The extension through the hips should carry the body well away from the bar, finishing in swing down to a hang.

1. THROW UPWARD AND AWAY FROM BAR WITH CONFIDENCE.

2. EXTEND WELL THROUGH ARMS AND SHOULDERS.

3. ALLOW HIPS TO RISE AS HIGH AS POSSIBLE BEFORE EXTENDING THROUGH HIPS.

4. WORK FOR MAXIMUM ROTATION RATHER THAN DROP.

5. MAINTAIN HEAD POSITION BETWEEN THE ARMS DURING THE SWING.

Combined Grasp Cast

Grasp the bar in a combined grasp. Develop a small swing. As the body begins to swing forward, pull vigorously on the bar, bending the arms enough for the top of the head to rise bar level. At this moment pike sharply at the hips, lifting the legs close to the bar. As the knees approach the bar, extend upward and outward through the hips. Simultaneously push against the bar by extending the arms.

Complete the extension through the body prior to beginning the back swing. Allow the body to swing freely through to a high back swing.

1. BEGIN WITH A SMALL SWING.
2. DRAW LEGS CLOSE TO BAR FOR CAST.
3. PULL SHARPLY WITH ARMS WHEN INITIATING CAST.
4. DRIVE FEET WELL ABOVE BAR DURING CAST.
5. KEEP HIPS CLOSE TO BAR WHEN EXTENDING THROUGH HIPS AND ARMS.
6. HOLD BODY STRAIGHT FOLLOWING HIP EXTENSION.

Cast One-Half Turn

Start from a straight arm support position backward, pushing the bar from the thighs to the ankles. Maintain this piked position with the ankles against the bar as you swing under it. Drive the hips forward and upward, extending them toward the top of the swing.

The left arm pulls during the turn. As you complete the turn, the right hand reaches in with a regular grip. Swing forward under the bar with a mixed grip. At the peak of the front swing, stretch forward with the shoulders and change the undergrip hand to a regular grip.

1. **DEVELOP ABDOMINAL MUSCLES AND HIP FLEXORS TO KEEP YOUR ANKLES AGAINST BAR DURING PIKE SWING.**

2. **AS YOU SWING UNDER THE BAR, DRIVE HIPS UPWARD.**

3. **TOWARD THE PEAK OF SWING, EXTEND HIPS OUT TO LEFT TO FACILITATE TURN.**

4. **REGRASP WITH LEFT HAND IN REGULAR GRIP.**

Stem Rise

Jump to the bar grasping it in a reverse grip. Swing forward by raising the legs forward and outward. Maintain a stretched body position as you swing back.

At the end of the short, stretched back swing, lift the heels backward, pulling the chest toward the bar.

Hold this straight body pull-up position for a fraction of a second then lean back, piking at the hips and straightening the arms. Watch the bar.

After your shoulders pass through the bottom of the swing, extend your hips upward into a handstand and press down with your arms. Swing down in a stretched position, straight from wrists to ankles.

1. **WAIT FOR THE VERY END OF BACK SWING BEFORE DOING PULL UP.**

2. **STRAIGHTEN OUT YOUR ARMS AS YOU PIKE.**

3. **WATCH BAR UNTIL MOVE IS COMPLETED TO HANDSTAND.**

4. **DRIVE HIPS AND FEET UPWARD, PUSHING DOWN WITH ARMS.**

Cast to Handstand, Reverse Grip

Start from a support position with hands in reverse grip. Bend forward, bringing the bar from the thighs to the waist. Shoulders and legs fold toward one another and arms are bent slightly. Drive the heels backward and upward, pushing downward with the arms.

As your body rises slightly past a handstand, the arms straighten. Eyes are focused on the bar.

From this stretched position duck your head into a neutral position, swinging forward in the direction of the heel drive. The body swings down in a stretched position, straight from wrists to ankles.

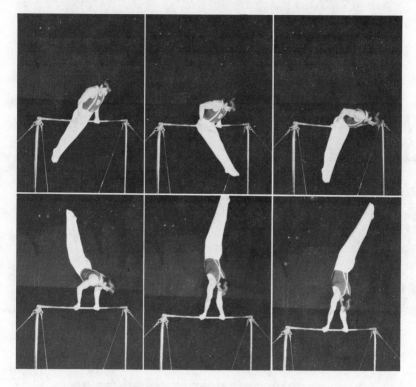

1. PRACTICE PRESS HANDSTANDS AND HANDSTAND DIPS ON FLOOR TO STRENGTHEN ARMS FOR PUSHING ACTION.

2. BEND ARMS JUST ENOUGH TO ALLOW BAR TO COME TO YOUR WAIST WHEN YOU FOLD OVER IT.

3. A POWERFUL UPWARD HEEL DRIVE AND STRONG DOWNWARD PUSH WITH ARMS ARE NECESSARY TO FINISH CAST TO A HANDSTAND POSITION.

4. AVOID ARCHING AS IT WILL HAVE A NEGATIVE EFFECT ON THE SWING WHICH WILL FOLLOW THE HANDSTAND.

Cast to Handstand, Regular Grip

Start from a support position with hands in a regular grip. Bend forward bringing the bar from the thighs to the waist. Shoulders and legs fold toward each other and the arms bend slightly.

Drive the heels backward and upward, pushing downward with the arms. As the body rises almost to a handstand, the arms straighten. Eyes are focused on the bar and remain there for the swing down. Body is stretched straight from wrists to ankles as you swing down toward the direction from which you cast.

1. PRACTICE PRESS HANDSTANDS AND HANDSTAND DIPS ON FLOOR TO STRENGTHEN ARMS FOR PUSHING ACTION.

2. BEND ARMS JUST ENOUGH TO ALLOW BAR TO COME TO YOUR WAIST WHEN YOU FOLD OVER IT.

3. A POWERFUL UPWARD HEEL DRIVE AND STRONG DOWNWARD PUSH WITH ARMS ARE NECESSARY TO FINISH CAST TO A HANDSTAND POSITION.

4. AVOID ARCHING AS IT WILL HAVE A NEGATIVE EFFECT ON THE SWING WHICH WILL FOLLOW THE HANDSTAND.

short circles

Single Leg Rise

Grasp the bar in regular grip and initiate a medium swing. As the body reaches the extent of its forward swing, stretch the shoulders, pressing back with the hands. Pike at the waist, bringing the ankles toward the bar and scooping one leg through.

Drive the leg upward at a 45-degree angle to the floor after the center of gravity passes under the bar.

Arms press down just after the leg drive begins. Bar moves from the bottom of the legs to the top to finish in a support position.

1. **REMEMBER TO STRETCH SHOULDERS FORWARD BEFORE SCOOPING THROUGH WITH LEG.**

2. **LEG DRIVE OR HIP EXTENSION BEGINS AFTER CENTER OF GRAVITY PASSES UNDER BAR.**

3. **PULL WITH STRAIGHT ARMS DURING LEG DRIVE.**

Single Knee Circle Backward

To get into the starting position, grasp the bar in regular grip and perform a pull over to support. Press off one hand and cut the leg which is on that side to the front position. Regrasp the bar outside the leg. Bend the front leg to a 90-degree angle.

From this starting position press down with the shoulders, keeping the arms straight so that the bent leg is no longer in contact with the bar. The other leg is extended backward.

Bring the back of the front knee to the bar, simultaneously leaning back and kicking the opposite leg forward. The back of the knee is kept on the bar throughout the rest of the swing. The body swings through the bottom and as it rises in front, lift the chest upward and shift the wrists on top of the bar.

1. ONCE IN POSITION TO START THE MOVEMENT, KEEP BACK LEG STRAIGHT AND FORWARD LEG BENT TO ABOUT A 90-DEGREE ANGLE.

2. TO START DOWNWARD SWING SHIFT BACK, LEANING SHOULDERS BACKWARD AND AWAY FROM BAR. DON'T LOOK BACK.

3. KEEP BACK OF BENT KNEE AGAINST BAR. LONG PANTS HELP PREVENT ABRASIONS.

4. TOWARD LAST PART OF KNEE CIRCLE, REMEMBER TO SHIFT WRISTS ON TOP OF THE BAR.

Double Knee Circle Backward

Start from a sitting position on the bar with the hands in a regular grip on either side of the legs. Bend both knees to a 90-degree angle, pressing down with the shoulders and extending the arms. Shift back bringing the back of the knees to the bar and then lean back with the shoulders. After passing through the bottom of the swing, lift forward and upward with the chest and shift the wrists on top of the bar.

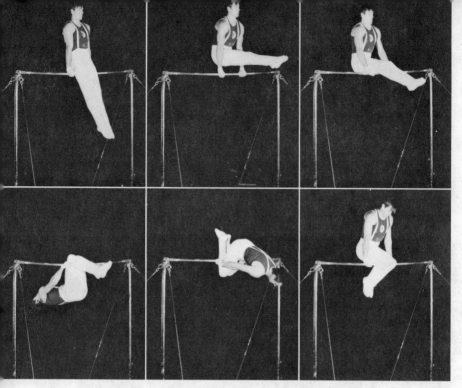

1. **BEND LEGS TO FORM 90-DEGREE ANGLE.**

2. **SHIFT BACK TO START DOWNWARD SWING BY LEANING SHOULDERS AWAY FROM BAR. DON'T LOOK BACK.**

3. **KEEP BACK OF KNEES BENT AGAINST BAR.**

4. **SHIFT WRIST TO TOP OF BAR DURING LAST PART OF CIRCLE.**

Back Seat Circle

Start from a sitting position on the bar with the hands in regular grip on either side of the legs. Straighten the legs and arms to hold a momentary "L" position with the bar below the knees.

Press the shoulders back, piking deeper by collapsing your legs in toward your face as your body swings down.

After the center of gravity passes through the bottom of the swing, open the chest upward, shifting the wrists on top of the bar. Finish in a sitting position on top of the bar.

1. DO NOT LOOK BACK WITH YOUR HEAD.

2. KEEP ARMS STRAIGHT.

3. MAINTAIN DEEP PIKE AS YOU SWING DOWN WITH ARMS PASSING BY KNEES.

4. OPEN OUT OF PIKE JUST AFTER SHOULDERS PASS THROUGH BOTTOM OF SWING.

5. DURING THE "OPEN OUT," CONCENTRATE ON LIFTING CHEST FORWARD AND UPWARD WHILE KEEPING HIPS IN PLACE.

Rear Rise

With the hands in an overgrasp, develop a medium swing from a hang. During the forward swing, extend through the shoulders while pressing away from the bar. Hollow slightly through the back.

As the first swing approaches its maximum height and begins its backward motion, pike sharply, bringing both ankles toward the bar. At this moment pass the legs between the arms and hands. Keep the legs straight.

When the height of the backward swing is reached, press down on the bar and lift through the shoulders and chest. The downward action of the legs toward the chest should result in an action against the bar which pulls the shoulders upward. Continue to force the shoulders and chest forward and upward to finish in a seat support on top of the bar.

1. **WHEN PASSING THE LEGS BETWEEN THE HANDS, DROP THROUGH THE HIPS AND EXTEND THROUGH THE SHOULDERS.**

2. **PASS THE FEET BETWEEN THE ARMS BEFORE THE HIPS PASS UNDER BAR ON RETURN SWING.**

3. **EXECUTE A SHARP FLEXION OF HIPS.**

4. **KEEP HANDS ABOUT SHOULDER'S-WIDTH APART.**

Straddle Rise

This movement is similar to the rear rise. With an overgrasp in the hang position, swing forward holding the back slightly hollow. On the backward swing, pike sharply, bringing the ankles towards the bar. Simultaneously straddle the arms with the legs.

As the shoulders begin their backward motion and prior to the hips' passing under the bar, project the feet under the bar. Allow the leg to fold onto the chest.

As the reaction from the bar pulls on the hands, extend through the hips while pressing down on the bar. Lift the shoulders and chest forward and upward. Finish in a straddle seat position on top of the bar.

1. KEEP LEGS STRAIGHT THROUGHOUT THE MOVEMENT.
2. BEGIN THE RISE WITH LEGS TOGETHER THEN STRADDLE LATER.
3. BEGIN WITH HANDS CLOSE TOGETHER.
4. MAINTAIN STRAIGHT ARMS.
5. THINK OF MOVEMENT AS A CIRCLE ACTION.

Backward Hip Circle

From a front support with an overgrasp, bend the arms slightly until the stomach touches the bar and the legs are under the bar. Press down, straightening the arms and simultaneously swinging the legs backward and upward.

As the legs swing forward approaching the bar, press away with the arms, shifting the body action onto the shoulders. Maintain a straight body and swing the legs around and up the other side of the bar. The hands rotate around the bar slightly leading the body rotation.

A sharp wrist shift around the bar allows you to finish the movement in a free front support. As the shoulders pass below the bar, a slight tug is felt on the hand. At this moment stretch through the hips and lean well onto the shoulders.

1. **WAIT UNTIL SHOULDERS SWING UNDER BAR BEFORE EXTENDING AT HIPS.**
2. **KEEP LEGS STRAIGHT.**
3. **USE TUG ON HANDS TO LIFT HIPS AND SHOULDERS.**
4. **KEEP ARMS STRAIGHT THROUGHOUT.**
5. **LEAN WELL BACK ONTO THE SHOULDERS.**

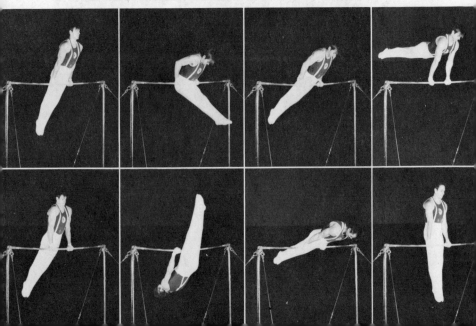

Forward Hip Circle

Grasp the bar in regular grip and take a support position. Straighten the arms so that the thighs rest against the bar. Lean forward at the shoulders, keeping the body straight as you fall forward and downward. The thighs remain pressed against the bar.

When the body is about parallel to the floor, pike deeply, shifting your weight around to the top of the bar. The shoulders lean around the bar and the arms and body straighten simultaneously as you finish in a support position.

1. BODY SHOULD BE STRAIGHT OR SLIGHTLY ARCHED AS FORWARD FALL BEGINS.

2. HANDS SHOULD HAVE A LOOSE GRASP SO THAT THEY MAY BE ROTATED EASILY DURING THE PIKE.

3. DURING THE HAND ROTATION, THIGHS STAY IN CONTACT WITH BAR. IF THIGHS ARE NOT KEPT AGAINST BAR, BODY WILL FALL AWAY.

4. CONCENTRATE ON LEAVING LEGS WHERE THEY ARE AND BENDING CHEST AROUND.

Forward Seat Circle

Sit on the bar, grasping it in a reverse grip. Press the legs into an "L" and lift the hips upward so that the arms are to either side of the knees. Lean forward, pressing away with the shoulders and pulling the legs against the chest so that you are in the deepest pike possible.

Hold this position until you pass under the bar. As you feel the reaction of the bar, pull the arms backward. Toward the top of the swing extend the hips and finish in a sitting position on the bar.

1. **TRY TO GET INTO DEEPEST PIKE POSSIBLE BEFORE FALLING FORWARD. BACK SHOULD BE ROUNDED AND KEPT THAT WAY THROUGH BOTTOM OF SWING.**

2. **KEEP ARMS STRAIGHT AND SHOULDERS PRESSED AWAY FROM THE BAR DURING ENTIRE CIRCLE.**

3. **BAR WILL REACT AFTER YOU PASS THROUGH BOTTOM. WHEN IT DOES, PULL BACK WITH ARMS.**

Backward Straddle Circle

Take a support position with hands in closer than a shoulder's-width apart and in regular grip. Cast up toward a handstand. As the body drops, straddle your legs toward your ears, pressing back with your shoulders. Eyes watch the bar. Pass through the bottom of the swing with the back rounded and shoulders pressed away.

After passing through the bottom, the shoulders rise as a reaction to the bottoming effect of the bar. Lift the hips upward, press down with the arms and shift the wrists to the top of the bar. Allow the hips to drop down to finish in a straddle sitting position.

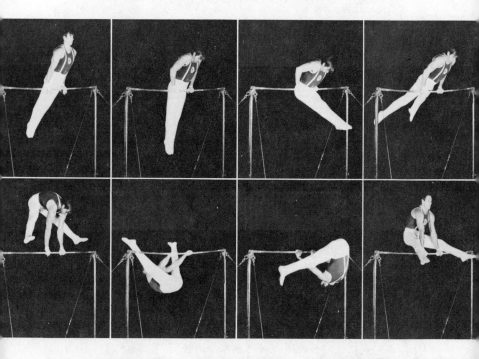

1. WATCH BAR DURING THE ENTIRE STRADDLE CIRCLE.
2. HOLD STRADDLE PIKE AS DEEP AS POSSIBLE KEEPING YOUR SHOULDERS PRESSED AWAY FROM BAR FOR A BETTER SWING.
3. AFTER YOU PASS THROUGH BOTTOM OF SWING, LIFT HIPS AND PULL DOWN WITH ARMS.

Forward Sole Circle (Straddled)

This movement is a short circle with the soles of the feet placed on either side of the hands and the legs, a little more than a shoulder's-width apart.

From a front support with an undergrasp, thrust up and away from the bar. Lift the hips sharply by pressing away through the shoulders. Keep the legs straight and place the soles of the feet upon the bar on the outside of the hands. At this moment fall forward and lean well into circle. Press away with the arms to make the radius of the circle as long as possible.

As the circle action of the body is gaining momentum, press the chest toward the legs and bring the chin toward the chest. Finish the circle on top of the bar.

1. **LEAN WELL ONTO SHOULDERS.**
2. **PRESS ONTO BAR WITH FEET.**
3. **MAINTAIN A FIRM HIP POSITION AS BODY PASSES BELOW BAR.**
4. **KEEP BODY STRAIGHT FROM SHOULDERS TO TOES.**

Backward Sole Circle (Straddled)

This movement is similar to that of the front sole circle. The overgrip is taken while the body is held in a front support.

Shift the shoulders slightly forward of the hands while bending the arms and allowing the legs to swing slightly forward of the hands and below the bar. Thrust from the bar by straightening the arms and pressing the body upward and backward. Pike sharply at the hips, simultaneously placing the soles of the feet on the bar outside of the hands.

Press the shoulders back and deepen the pike. Shift the body weight onto the shoulders while pulling the feet against the bar. Keep the arms straight and lean to the rear.

Hold the hips firm and legs straight throughout the circle. Finish the movement in a straddle stand on top of the bar.

1. **PRESS WELL AWAY FROM BAR WITH SHOULDERS.**
2. **CLOSE PIKE DURING UPWARD PART OF CIRCLE.**
3. **KEEP LEGS STRAIGHT THROUGHOUT.**
4. **PULL AGAINST BAR TO MAINTAIN FOOT-BAR CONTACT.**

kip movements

Kip

Grasp the bar in regular grip and initiate a swing. As the body reaches the extent of its forward swing, stretch the shoulders, pressing back with your hands. Pike at the waist, drawing the ankles to the bar.

As the center of gravity passes under the bar, extend the hips at a 45-degree angle and press down with straight arms. The bar moves along the legs to the thighs so that you come to a straight arm support position.

1. KEEP ARMS STRAIGHT THROUGHOUT ENTIRE MOVEMENT. DO NOT PUMP SWING PRECEDING KIP; INSTEAD, LET MOMENTUM CARRY FORWARD AND CONCENTRATE ON STRETCHING AWAY FROM BAR.

2. ANKLES ARE BROUGHT TO BAR AT FORWARDMOST PART OF SWING JUST BEFORE BACKWARD SWING BEGINS.

3. WAIT UNTIL SHOULDERS PASS THROUGH
   BOTTOM OF SWING BEFORE EXTENDING HIPS.

4. HIP EXTENSION BEGINS FRACTION OF SECOND
   BEFORE THE STRAIGHT ARM PULL.

Drop Kip

Start in a straight arm support position with regular grip. Press the hips and shoulders backward, pushing the bar from the thighs to the ankles. Maintain the pike position with the ankles against the bar as you swing upward in front.

Ankles are held against the bar as the swing back begins. The center of gravity passes under the bar, you extend the hips at a 45-degree angle and press down with the arms to finish in a support position.

1. **TENDENCY IS FOR ANKLES TO MOVE AWAY FROM BAR ON THE FORWARD AND UPWARD SWING. HOLD THEM RIGIDLY AGAINST BAR BY KEEPING HIP FLEXORS AND ABDOMINALS TIGHT.**

Back Kip

Grasp the bar with a regular grip and initiate a medium swing. As the body reaches the extent of its forward swing, stretch the shoulders, pressing backward with the arms.

Pike at the waist, scooping the legs under the bar. As you rise in back, extend the hips upward while pressing down with the arms.

After the hips and shoulders rise to their full height, start to swing down. Collapse the legs in toward your face. As you swing under the bar, you should be in the deepest pike possible. When center of gravity passes through the bottom of the swing, open the chest upward, shifting the wrists on top of the bar. Finish in a sitting position on top of the bar.

1. EXECUTE LAST PART OF THIS MOVE IN A MANNER SIMILAR TO THAT OF BACK SEAT CIRCLE.

combined circles

Back Uprise

This movement involves transferring the body from an underswing to a free front support followed by a circle backwards.

With the hands in an overgrasp, execute a high, under-bar cast. When the body swings backward while passing under the bar, press downward with the arms and simultaneously pull into the bar. Keep the arms straight and hollow slightly through the hips. Keep the legs from swinging backward too far by checking through the hips.

When the legs pass under the bar, execute a sharp flick of the heels. As the shoulders begin to rise and hips approach the bar, keep the body straight. Shift the circle action onto the shoulders by leaning back while holding firm with the hands. Finish the movement with a back hip circle to a front support.

1. **KEEP ARMS STRAIGHT AND PRESS DOWN VIGOROUSLY.**
2. **BEGIN WITH A HIGH, UNDER-BAR CAST.**
3. **CONTROL HEIGHT OF LEGS ON BACK UNDERSWING.**
4. **DURING THE RISE, SHIFT HANDS WELL OVER BAR.**
5. **EXECUTE A SHARP HEEL WHIP.**

Sole Circle Cast
One-Half Turn

Begin this movement like the sole circle backward. As the shoulders pass below the bar and the hips begin to rise, extend the hips and remove the feet from the bar. At this moment twist at the hips and press away with the arms.

As the hips reach their full extension, release the bar with the right hand. Continue to press away with the pivot arm. Circle the right hand around under the bar and regrasp the bar with an overgrip outside the left hand. Square the shoulders with the bar and continue the swing under the bar.

1. **KEEP HANDS APART A SHOULDER'S-WIDTH OR LESS.**
2. **MAINTAIN A NARROW STRADDLE POSITION.**
3. **RETAIN GRASP WITH BOTH HANDS AS LONG AS POSSIBLE TO GAIN MAXIMUM UPWARD SHOULDER LIFT.**
4. **KEEP PIVOT ARM STRAIGHT.**
5. **SQUEEZE LEGS TOGETHER.**
6. **EXTEND WELL THROUGH HIPS FOR TWIST.**

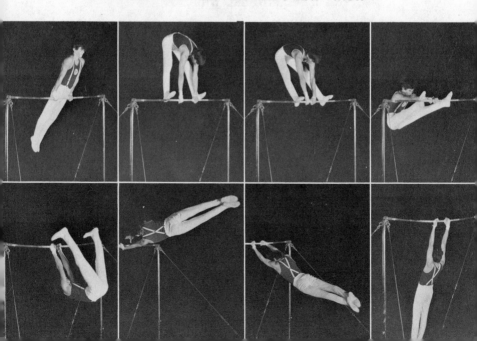

Free Hip Circle
Backward to Handstand

From a front support with an overgrasp, bend the arms slightly allowing the stomach to touch the bar while the legs pass below and forward of the hands. With a vigorous push downward on the bar, thrust the legs backward and upward. This should create a high swing up from the bar.

As the body returns back toward the bar, lean onto the shoulders, creating rotation about the shoulders. Maintain straight arms and a slight pike through the hips. As the legs circle under the bar and the shoulders drop backward, hold the body pike until a tug on the hands and arms is felt.

The action of the bar begins to lift the body up and away from the bar. At this moment extend through the hips and shoot up into a handstand. Finish the movement in the handstand.

1. HOLD PIKE POSITION UNTIL ARM TUG IS FELT.
2. KEEP ARMS STRAIGHT THROUGHOUT.
3. KEEP FIRM GRASP ON BAR. MAINTAIN HEAD-BODY ALIGNMENT.
4. SHIFT WRISTS TO TOP OF BAR, SLIGHTLY AHEAD OF THE BODY LIFT.

Kreis Kehre

This movement involves a half turn over the bar to a straddle support. With the hands in a combined grasp, execute a high cast swing. As the body passes below the bar, begin a backup rise movement. When the shoulders rise above the bar and the hips begin to approach the bar, transfer the body weight over and onto the arm with the hand in the undergrasp. Press away with the arm and begin to straddle one leg sideways.

When the shoulders are positioned above the bar, release the overgrasp hand, simultaneously rotate through the shoulders and regrasp the bar to the far side of the support arm. Push and extend vigorously with the support arm. At this moment circle the leg on top of the bar and to the far side of the support arm.

Finish the movement in a straddle support with both hands in an overgrasp. During the straddle, press away with both arms, holding a high straddle support.

1. **LIFT HIGH THROUGH HIPS WHEN INITIATING STRADDLE.**

2. **KEEP SHOULDERS DIRECTLY OVER HANDS.**

3. **PRESS VIGOROUSLY AGAINST BAR WITH PIVOT ARM.**

4. **KEEP ARMS STRAIGHT.**

5. **LEAD TURN WITH THE HEAD AND SHOULDERS.**

Dislocate

Start in a sitting position with the body arched and the hands in a reverse grip. Drive your legs in toward your face, pressing your hips off the bar. This places you in a deep pike position. Drive the legs up and out, pressing back with the shoulders and arms. The head drops back and you dislocate at the shoulders.

Swing down with the body straight and with the hands in an eagle grip.

Swing up in back. At the peak of the backward swing, press down with the arms, to release the bar and regrasp in a regular grip.

1. SHOULDERS NEED TO BE FLEXIBLE SO BE SURE YOU HAVE PRACTICED APPROPRIATE EXERCISES UNDER THE FLEXIBILITY SECTION.

2. THIS MOVE MAY BE EXECUTED FROM A FORWARD SEAT CIRCLE.

3. YOU MAY DO A BACK UPRISE OUT OF THE MOVE AND SHIFT YOUR HANDS TO REGULAR GRIP.

vault movements

Rear Vault

Execute a mixed grip cast and ride the swing as far as possible. As the momentum slows down, press down with the arms, pull the feet into an "L" position and turn the shoulders toward the hand in a reverse grip. Both arms pull down, but the regular grip hand takes more of the weight and pulls more vigorously.

The reverse grip hand is released first and as the body passes over the bar in a piked position.

Turn the shoulders regrasping the bar with both hands in a regular grip and extend the hips backward so that the entire body is stretched and in good position to swing down and under the bar.

1. AS SOON AS BACKWARD SWING STARTS, MOST OF WEIGHT SHOULD BE TRANSFERRED TO THE REGULAR GRIP HAND.

2. BODY SHOULD REMAIN STRETCHED UNTIL MOMENTUM SLOWS DOWN. THEN LIFT HEELS INTO AN "L" AND START TURNING.

3. REGULAR GRIP HAND THRUSTS AWAY AS BODY PASSES OVER BAR.

4. IF VAULT WAS EXECUTED PROPERLY, BODY CAN BE TURNED QUICKLY ENOUGH TO RE-GRASP SIMULTANEOUSLY WITH BOTH HANDS.

5. STRETCH BACKWARD AFTER REGRASPING.

6. HAVE A PERSON SPOT YOU ON THE OTHER SIDE OF THE BAR TO STAND IN A POSITION WHERE YOUR LEGS WILL TURN AWAY FROM HIM DURING THE VAULT.

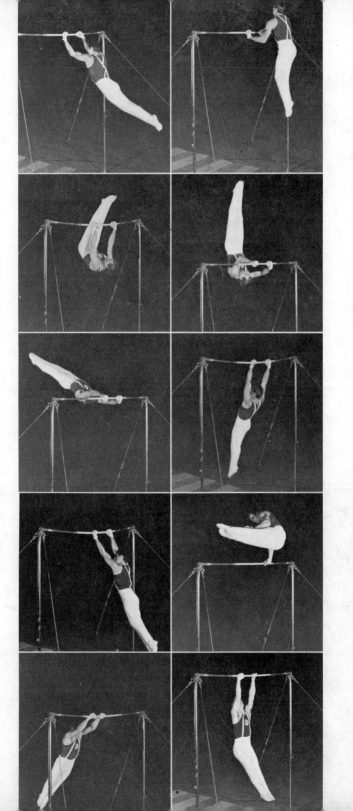

Flank Cut

Grasp the bar in a regular grip and initiate a medium swing. As the body reaches the extent of its forward swing, stretch the shoulders, pressing backward with the arms. Pike at the waist, scooping the legs under the bar.

As you rise in back, hold the pike until you are almost to the peak of the backswing. Extend your hips upward, pressing down with the arms. The bar moves from knee to hip level.

One hand releases and the hips turn around it as the legs cut to the side. Regrasp the bar with a regular grip as soon as the legs pass the bar and extend the hips backward so that the body is completely stretched before passing through the bottom of the swing.

1. WORK ON HAMSTRING FLEXIBILITY AND ABDOMINAL MUSCLE STRENGTH SO THAT YOU CAN PERFORM THE STOOP IN.

2. RIDE BACKSWING AS HIGH AS POSSIBLE BEFORE EXTENDING AND PRESSING DOWN WITH ARMS.

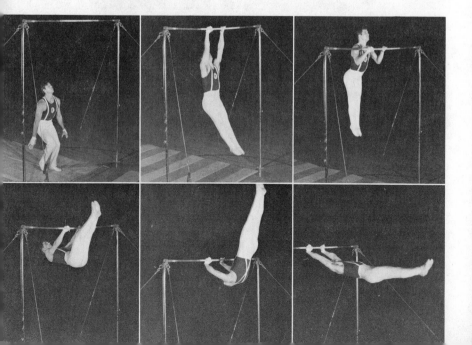

3. TURN HIPS WHILE KEEPING SHOULDERS AS
   SQUARE AS POSSIBLE DURING THE LEG CUT.

4. UNLESS YOU CATCH EARLY AND EXTEND HIPS
   BACKWARD, YOU WILL NOT GET A GOOD SWING.

long circles

Three-Quarter Back Giant

The beginning of this movement involves the same technique as that for the cast backward to a long underswing. The cast should be well above the bar. During the downswing the body must be extended from hands to feet. The head takes a position between the arms. As the legs pass below the bar, a scooping action is essential to create the needed momentum for the movement.

Following the leg beat, hollow slightly through the hips simultaneously glancing at the bar. While keeping the arms straight, press against the bar with the hands and bring the hips to the bar.

As the legs begin to swing over the bar, quickly shift the wrist, placing the hands in a support position on top of the bar. The hand action should lead the body rotation.

Finish the movement with a back hip circle coming to a front leaning rest support position.

1. **CAST AWAY WITH STRAIGHT ARMS.**
2. **CAST HIGH AND EXTEND THROUGH HIPS.**
3. **SCOOP WITH FORCE THROUGH BOTTOM OF SWING.**
4. **FOCUS ON BAR PRIOR TO MAKING CONTACT.**

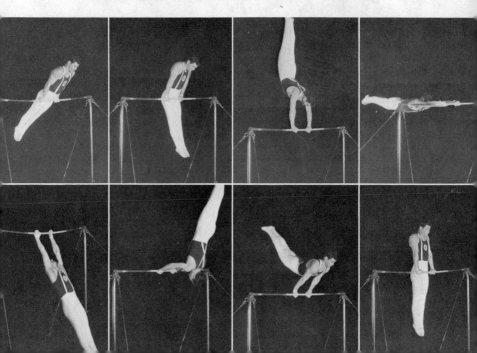

Three-Quarter Front Giant

Start from a support position with hands in a reverse grip. Cast into a straight, stretched and slightly overbalanced handstand.

As you fall forward duck your head into a neutral position. Maintain a straight body throughout the entire downward swing.

When the body rises halfway to the horizontal in the backward swing, round the back. Momentum carries you to a three-quarter handstand position.

Pull the shoulders over the bar, shifting the hands to a regular grip and allowing the body to swing down to complete the move in a straight arm support position.

1. **AFTER CASTING TO A STRAIGHT HANDSTAND, ALLOW BODY TO FALL WITH THE HELP OF GRAVITY AND YOU WILL COAST TO THE THREE-QUARTER HANDSTAND POSITION.**

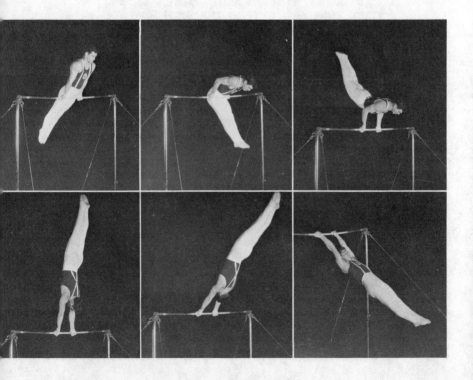

Backward Giant

This movement is rotation around the bar at full arm and body length. With the hands in an overgrasp and the body in a front leaning support position on the bar, cast upward into a handstand on top of the bar. Keep the body straight and extend through the chest and shoulders as the downward movement begins.

As the bottom of the downward swing is approached, scoop with the feet, whipping the legs vigorously forward and upward. Keep the head positioned between the arms. This slight shortening of the body length provides the essential added upward momentum to carry the body up and over the bar.

As the handstand is approached, extend through the hips and shoulders while shifting the hands on top of the bar. The leg scoop and hip flick are two essential techniques which must be mastered for successful giant swings. If the hip whip followed by the hip and shoulder extension is properly timed, there will be a slight pause when passing through the handstand.

1. CAST WELL INTO A HANDSTAND.

2. EXTEND WELL THROUGH ARMS, SHOULDERS AND HIPS.

3. FLICK VIGOROUSLY THROUGH HIPS TO ACHIEVE MAXIMUM UPWARD MOMENTUM.

4. BEGIN BODY EXTENSION PRIOR TO RETURNING TO HANDSTAND POSITION ON TOP OF BAR.

5. ESTABLISH A RHYTHM TO EXTEND, SCOOP AND EXTEND AS THE CIRCLE IS COMPLETED.

Forward Giant

Start from a support position with hands in a reverse grip. Cast into a straight, stretched and slightly overbalanced handstand.

As you fall forward, duck your head into a neutral position. Maintain a straight body position throughout the entire downward swing and halfway to the horizontal during the upward swing. Hips pike very slightly and the back rounds out. Eyes focus on the bar. Shoulders continue to press away as you rise to a three-quarter handstand position with the body slightly piked.

Extend the hips upward and pass over the bar in a straight body position, ducking the head into a neutral position during the downward swing.

1. **CAST TO A SLIGHTLY OVERBALANCED BUT STRAIGHT HANDSTAND.**

2. **RIDE SWING UNTIL HALFWAY TO THE HORIZONTAL ON BACKWARD SWING. SLIGHT PIKE IN THE BODY WILL SPEED UP YOUR ROTATION SO THAT YOU WILL HAVE ENOUGH MOMENTUM TO CARRY YOU OVER THE TOP.**

3. **EXTEND INTO A STRETCHED POSITION BEFORE REACHING TOP OF THE GIANT AND PASS OVER THE BAR IN THE STRETCHED POSITION.**

Backward Giant, Cross Change

Begin from a back giant circle with the hands in an overgrasp. As the body passes over the top of the bar, release one hand to cross over the other.

Extend well through the shoulders, keeping the arms extended. As the downward swing begins, keep the shoulders square with the bar. This position should be held as long as possible through the swing.

As the swing passes below the bar, scoop and whip with the legs. At this moment the body tends to turn; therefore, release the under hand to regrasp the bar in an undergrasp.

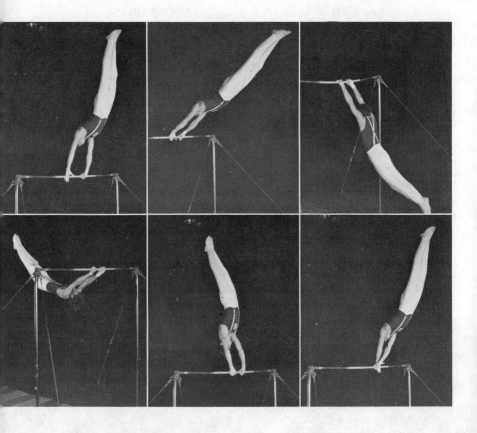

1. **EXECUTE CHANGE INTO A CROSS GRIP AS BODY PASSES OVER TOP OF BAR.**

2. **MAINTAIN STRAIGHT ARMS.**

3. **TWIST WITH SCOOP AND HIP EXTENSION ACTION.**

4. **HOLD CROSS GRIP AS LONG AS POSSIBLE.**

Overgrasp Change to Front Giant

This movement is often referred to as a *blind change.*

Begin the movement from a back giant circle with the hands in an overgrasp. As the body passes over the top of the bar, move the hands together, thereby swinging downward in a close grasp. Execute the normal leg and hip action as in the regular back giant.

When the upward motion begins, extend through the hips and begin the hip rotation necessary for the turn. Retain the overgrasp with both hands as long as possible.

As the body rises up to the handstand, rotate through the shoulders, simultaneously releasing one hand. Complete the rotation on the pivot arm, replacing the released hand in an undergrasp as the body passes over the top of the bar in a handstand.

1. TURN AS LATE AS POSSIBLE.
2. PRESS AWAY WITH PIVOT ARM THROUGH SHOULDERS.
3. RETAIN OVERGRASP AS LONG AS POSSIBLE.
4. INITIATE TURN WITH HIPS.
5. KEEP ARMS EXTENDED AT ALL TIMES.

Half Pirouette Forward

Execute one or two forward giant swings to build up momentum. When the body rises halfway to the horizontal on the backward swing, begin the pike just as in a normal giant swing. Pull more with the left arm, transferring the weight to that arm. Head and shoulders lead the turn.

When you are three-quarters of the way to a handstand, extend out of the pike and rotate the hips into the turn. The right hand is released and completes the turn to a handstand. The right hand regrasps in a regular grip and you stretch away from the bar in preparation for a backward giant swing.

1. **LEARN MOVE BY CASTING UP TO A HANDSTAND THEN PIROUETTING ON A LOW BAR.**

2. **WHEN WORKING OUT OF THE GIANT SWINGS, REMEMBER TO TURN EARLY. OTHERWISE YOU WON'T HAVE TIME TO COMPLETE THE TURN AND YOU WILL SWING DOWN CROOKEDLY.**

3. **YOU NEED A GOOD INITIAL GIANT SWING TO HAVE ENOUGH MOMENTUM TO CARRY YOU OVER THE BAR WHEN YOU TURN EARLY.**

4. **ALWAYS LEAD THE TURN WITH HEAD AND SHOULDERS FOLLOWED BY HIPS.**

dismounts

Squat Dismount

Start from a support position with hands in regular grip. While keeping your shoulders in front of the bar cast into a three-quarter arched handstand position. Snap the legs down toward your chest and bend your knees. Simultaneously, push down with the arms and release with the hands.

When your feet clear the bar, extend the hips, lifting arms and chest upward and landing on the mat in an erect position.

1. **PRACTICE ON A LOW BAR WITH SPOTTER.**

2. **CAST INTO AN ARCHED THREE-QUARTER HANDSTAND TO MAKE THE SNAP DOWN EASIER.**

3. **SNAP DOWN VIGOROUSLY.**

4. **KEEP ARMS RIGIDLY LOCKED SO THAT BAR PRESSES DOWN WITH YOUR FORCE AND THEN SPRINGS BACK DURING YOUR RELEASE.**

5. **EXTEND FINGERS UPON RELEASE.**

6. **OPEN TO A STRETCHED POSITION AS SOON AS FEET CLEAR THE BAR.**

Straddle Dismount

Start in a support position with the hands in regular grip. Cast the legs above the shoulders, straddling them then snapping them down toward the end of the cast. At the same time your arms push off.

When your feet clear the bar, extend the hips, lifting your arms and chest upward to land on the mat in an erect position.

1. PRACTICE ON A LOW BAR WITH SPOTTER.
2. CAST INTO AN ARCHED THREE-QUARTER HANDSTAND TO MAKE THE SNAP DOWN EASIER.
3. SNAP DOWN VIGOROUSLY.
4. KEEP ARMS RIGIDLY LOCKED SO THAT BAR PRESSES DOWN WITH YOUR FORCE AND THEN SPRINGS BACK DURING YOUR RELEASE.
5. EXTEND FINGERS UPON RELEASE.
6. OPEN TO A STETCHED POSITION AS SOON AS FEET CLEAR THE BAR.

Giant Straddle Dismount

Grasp the bar in a reverse grip and pull over to a support.

Cast into a handstand and swing forward and under the bar. Ride the upward swing as long as possible. As your body begins to slow down, straddle your legs and lift your hips into a pike, simultaneously pulling the shoulders slightly over the bar.

As the legs pass over the bar, flick the wrists downward to release the bar.

After feet clear the bar, lift the arms and chest upward, finishing in a stand with back to the bar.

1. **DO NOT ATTEMPT WITHOUT SPOTTER.**
2. **AFTER CASTING TO HANDSTAND, RIDE SWING AS FAR AS POSSIBLE.**
3. **START PIKING AND STRADDLING AS YOU FEEL BODY SLOWING DOWN ON BACK-UPWARD SWING.**
4. **THROW BAR DOWN AND AFTER RELEASE, LIFT SHOULDERS.**

Sole Circle Dismount

From a front support with the hands in an over-grasp, bend the arms slightly, throwing the hips upward while keeping the shoulders slightly forward of the hands. Pike sharply at the hips, straddle the legs and place the feet on the bar outside of the hands. Extend the arms straight and lean back onto the shoulders. Press the feet firmly against the bar. Keep the legs extended from the hips. Lean backward allowing the body to circle backward under the bar.

As the shoulders rise to the far side of the bar, continue to press the feet against the bar. When the shoulders rise above the bar, release both hands and extend vigorously from the hips, thrusting the body upward and outward from the bar. At this moment stretch upward, lifting the arms overhead.

Quickly pike once more just prior to landing, thereby bringing the feet forward. Finish the movement in an upright standing position.

1. GAIN MAXIMUM DOWNWARD SWING BY
   EXTENDING HIPS BACKWARD AND PULLING
   CHIN TO CHEST.

2. KEEP LEGS ABOUT A SHOULDER'S-WIDTH
   APART WHEN STRADDLING ON THE BAR.

3. LOOK FOR FLOOR AS SHOULDERS RISE ON
   FAR SIDE OF BAR.

4. PRESS AWAY FIRMLY WITH FEET AS HANDS
   RELEASE GRASP.

Flyaway Dismount

It is essential that the basic swing be mastered prior to learning the backward somersault from a forward swing.

From a cast with an overgrasp, swing downward with a straight body. As the legs swing under the bar, pike slightly. At this moment extend from the pike and scoop vigorously with the feet, thereby whipping the legs sharply forward. When a tug is felt on the hands, extend upward and outward with the hips and legs. The whip against the bar should be felt just after the swing passes under the bar.

As the hip flick occurs, release the bar while watching the toes rise. Check the head position, keeping it aligned with the body. Throw the arms outward and sideward to shoulder level as the body rotates in the air. Rotation should be felt through the hips. Keep the body extended during the flight. Pike at the hips slightly, just prior to landing. Upon landing, bend the knees slightly and once again straighten them to finish the movement in an upright, standing position.

1. CAST HIGH, EXTENDING COMPLETELY THROUGH BODY.

2. SCOOP AT BOTTOM OF SWING.

3. FLICK VIGOROUSLY WITH LEGS ON UPSWING.

4. HOLD HEAD ALIGNED WITH BODY.

5. EXTEND THROUGH HIPS FOLLOWING LEG FLICK.

6. FEEL ROTATION THROUGH HIPS.

Dimensions

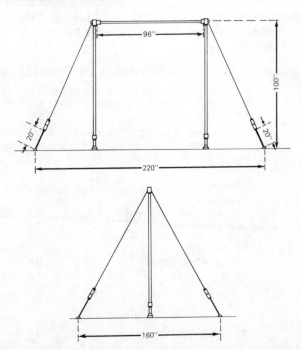

rules simplified

The horizontal bar exercise must consist exclusively of swinging without stops. One move must be performed with the back toward the bar. On the horizontal bar as well as on the rings, a gymnast may be assisted into the hang position, but he must maintain a correct posture from the moment his feet leave the floor, i.e., the evaluation of the gymnast's exercise begins the moment he leaves the floor.

The parts of the exercise must be connected in an elegant and fluid manner without superfluous movements, intermediate swings, repetitions of parts with the same succeeding or preceding connections, or parts which are too easy in relation to the rest of the exercise.

Spotting and assistance for prevention of accidents and moral support of the performer are permitted.

However, if assistance contributes to the success of a movement, a deduction of between 0.30 and 1.0 points may be made. In no case is the coach or any other official person allowed to speak with the gymnast during the performance of his exercise. If this happens, the gymnast is penalized from 0.10 to 0.30 points.

Positive or Negative Methods of Scoring

Judging may be done in one of two mathematical methods. One method awards points while the other subtracts deductions.

The practice of adding up the deductions and subtracting them from the point allotment for each category is referred to as *negative scoring*.

EXAMPLE:	POINTS ALLOWED	DEDUCTIONS
Difficulty	4.0	−0.5
Origin. & Value of Comb.	1.5	−0.8
Composition	0.5	−0.2
Execution	1.5	−0.8
Amplitude	1.5	−1.0
General Impression	1.0	−0.4
TOTAL	10.0	−3.7

The total 3.7 in deductions is subtracted from the possible 10.0 points to arrive at the final score for the gymnast of 6.3 points.

The method of awarding points to the gymnast in each of the categories according to how well she executed or met the requirements of that category is employing the technique of *positive scoring*.

EXAMPLE:	POINTS ALLOWED	POINTS AWARDED
Difficulty	4.0	3.5
Origin. & Value of Comb.	1.5	0.7
Composition	0.5	0.3
Execution	1.5	0.7
Amplitude	1.5	0.5
General Impression	1.0	0.6
TOTAL	10.0	6.3

The total of 6.3 points is the final score and would be used as the gymnast's score.

The negative method of scoring is best used to score an advanced, highly skilled gymnast. Obviously the better caliber gymnast will make fewer mistakes, and your mathematics will be much easier working with the small numbers of the few deductions.

Scoring information courtesy of National Federation of State High School Associations.

For Complete and Up-To-Date Rules and Scoring Information, Consult These Sources:

Amateur Athletic Union (AAU)
3400 W. 86th Street
Indianapolis, Indiana 46268

National Federation of State
High School Associations
P.O. Box 98
Elgin, Illinois 60120

conditioning for horizontal bar

Flexibility Training

Flexibility exercises are important for preventing injury and facilitating proper swing. Without adequate flexibility, many moves on the horizontal bar are impossible. When executing flexibility exercises for the shoulders, hamstrings and groin, stretch as far as you can go, hold for eight counts, exhale, relax, and then allow yourself to stretch further. Repeat several times.

Neck

Rolling head—Circle the head to the back, left side, front and right side. Alternate directions after several continuous circles.

Wrist

Rolling wrist—A loose fist is made with one hand while the opposite hand grasps it below the wrist. The wrist of the arm being held is circled. Alternate hands several times.

Pressing one hand against the other, place the palm of one hand against the fingers of the other and press the fingers back. Alternate hands several times.

Shoulders

Crab—Assume a long sitting position on the floor. Arms should be straight with hands on the mat. Bend knees, placing the bottom surface of the feet on the floor. Press stomach and hips upward so that a stretch is felt in the shoulders. Lower hips so they clear the floor. While keeping hands in place, walk feet forward and press shoulders in front of hands as far as they'll go.

Dislocate—With your back toward the low horizontal

bar, grasp it in a reverse grip. Walk your legs out, sliding the hands outward slightly. Put your head back and dislocate the shoulders so that you are now grasping the bar in an eagle grip. On future attempts keep the hands as close to a shoulder's-width apart as possible. When the shoulders achieve good flexibility, they should be able to dislocate providing the hands are a shoulder's-width apart.

Assume a push-up position—Bend at the waist, pressing the hips back and up and pressing the shoulders down toward the floor so that the stretch is felt in the shoulders. Rock back to the push-up position and repeat.

Hamstrings, Groin and Lower Back

Long sitting with chest on knees—Assume a long sitting position. Keep the legs straight and ankles plantar-flexed and reach for toes. Bend at waist and attempt to place the head on the legs, then the chest, and finally the stomach.

Straddle sitting—Assume a straddle sitting position with arms stretched forward. Attempt to place first the head, then the chest, and finally the stomach on the left leg.

Using the same technique, stretch toward the right leg and then toward the center area between the legs. Repeat several times. The back will be rounded for these exercises but later, as flexibility is gained, it will remain straighter.

Hip Ligaments and Tendons

Straddle forward and backward—Assume a straddle stand on the mat with the arms straight and hands planted on the floor in front of the hips.

1. While supporting much of the weight on the hands, slip the feet to the side as far as possible.

2. Walk the hands forward, keeping the feet in position, and then arch the hips toward the floor. Allow feet to slip to the side, only.

3. Walk hands back, place them behind the hips

and approach a straddle sitting position but don't allow the buttocks to touch the floor. Permit the feet to slip to the side, only.

Ankles

Sitting on ankles—Kneel on both knees with toes tucked under so that the ankles are plantar-flexed. Sit back onto heels, place hands behind hips, and bend at waist, pulling the knees off the mat and leaning back with the shoulders.

Dislocate—With your back toward the low horizontal bar, grasp it in a reverse grip. Walk your legs out, sliding the hands outward slightly. Put your head back and dislocate the shoulders so that you are now grasping the bar in an eagle grip.

On future attempts, keep the hands as close to a shoulder's-width apart as possible. When the shoulders achieve good flexibility they should be able to dislocate when the hands are a shoulder's-width apart.

Strength Training

Of the six international gymnastic events, the horizontal bar requires the least strength as it consists entirely of swing type movements. However, the muscles in the shoulders, arms, chest, hips and lower back are used frequently and need to be strong. The following exercises develop strength in these muscle groups.

Abdominal and Hip Flexor Exercise

V sits—Start in a supine position on the mat with arms behind head. Bend at waist, lifting straight legs and arms toward one another and touching the toes with the hands. Relax, allowing legs and arms to come back to mat.

Hang from the bar—Keep the legs straight to lift the ankles toward the bar. Repeat many times.

Handstand Dips

Kick up to a handstand against the wall. Bend the arms so that the top of the head barely touches the floor. Press back up. Repeat many times.

Heel Lifts

Start in a prone position with arms extended in front. Lift the heels and arms upward, keeping the legs and arms straight. Relax, allowing the hands and feet to contact the mat and repeat many times.

Pull Ups

Undergrip and/or overgrip—Start from a hang. Bend the arms and pull the chest to the bar. Allow the arms to straighten. Repeat many times.

suggested routines

Routine #1

1. Jump to double overgrasp hang.
2. Cast swing, kip to front support.
3. Cast to handstand, one and one-half back giant swings.
4. Lower to back hip circle, free back hip circle.
5. Drop kip, front hip circle.
6. Squat dismount.

Routine #2

1. Jump to combined grasp hang (right hand in undergrip).
2. Slight swing forward and backward, high cast forward to back uprise with one-half turn clockwise around right arm, swing left leg over bar to straddle in free support over bar (kreis kehre).
3. One and one-half backward straddle circles in free support, disengage legs and swing forward executing one-half turn to the right around right arm and regrasp left hand in an overgrip (cast

with one-half turn), swing forward and change left hand to undergrip.

4. Pass straight legs between hands and shoot to high rear rise for dislocate.

5. Back uprise to free support, changing to double overgrasp.

6. Backward free hip circle to handstand.

7. One and one-half giant swings backward, cross change.

8. Two front giant swings, straddle dismount.

Routine #3

1. Jump to combined grasp.

2. Pull to high cast, rear vault.

3. Kip to handstand, lower to bar and execute under bar cast with one-half turn to combined grasp.

4. Change to double undergrasp on front swing, immediate kip.

5. One and one-half forward giant swings, pirouette to back giant.

6. One and one-half back giant swings, overgrasp change to front giant swing (blind change).

7. One and one-half front giant swings, giant straddle dismount.

glossary of gymnastics terms

BACK: Abbreviated term for back somersault.

CAST: A term applied to projecting the body from one position to another as when extending the legs backward from a straight arm support position above the rings then pushing with the arms just prior to reaching the end of a backward swing.

DISMOUNT: The opposite of mount. A means of getting off the apparatus.

FLIP: Short term for somersault.

FORM: The grace and precision with which the performer executes a stunt or routine.

KNOCKOUT SYSTEM: Refers to man-to-man tournament competition where one performer must defeat another to advance toward the finals.

LAY OUT: A position in which the body is held straight, or slightly arched.

LOST: To become momentarily unaware of one's position during a stunt.

MOUNT: Method by which the performers get on their apparatus.

OPEN: To come out of a tuck or other closed position into a straight or less closed position.

PIKE: A position of the body in which the body is bent at the hips only. (Jackknife position)

PULL OVER: A ¾ somersault originating from a takeoff position, halfway between the seat and back, which carries the gymnast backwards around to his feet.

ROUTINE: A series of stunts.

SAVE: Used to describe an action in which a performer makes presentable an otherwise ruined stunt or routine.

SIDE: A slang term meaning Side Somersault.

SOMERSAULT: A turning of the body about an axis running through or near the hips (lateral or anterior-posterior). Any degree of revolution about such an axis may be classed as a somersault regardless of the position of the body at takeoff. A full somersault consists of body passage through 360 degrees, usually, but not necessarily, feet to feet.

SOMMY: Slang term for somersault.

SPOTTING: In practice sessions, this term applies to a person protecting and assisting the performer in the proper execution of a stunt. In competition, spotters stand ready to protect the performer in case of loss of control.

TUCK: A position of the body in which the knees and hips are tightly bent.

TURNOVER: Slang term for the somersault.

TWIST: A turning of the body about an axis passing through the center of the body from head to toe (longitudinal axis). Twists are often done in conjunction with one or more somersault motions, both motions being simultaneous or not, as the case may be.

TWISTER: Term describing twisting somersaults.

WRAP: A term used to describe the action of drawing the arms and elbows in close to the body to spin faster.

HORIZONTAL BAR

BACK UPRISE: From a hang, swing backward and rise to a support.

EAGLE GIANT: A giant executed with the arm rotated, palms out, and thumbs out.

FLANK VAULT: The performer releases the bar with both hands, vaults over the bar, turns and regrasps.

GERMAN GIANT: A cast backward from a sitting position with regular grip to a giant with an extended body.

KIPS: Moving from a piked position swing under the bar to a support above the bar by extending the body.

PIROUETTE: A half turn on top of the bar from reverse giants to regular giants.

REGULAR GIANT: A complete rotation around the bar in an extended position. Palms grip the bar in a regular grip with the thumbs pointing in.

REVERSE GIANT: Same as regular giant except done in an opposite direction with a reverse grip with thumbs pointing out.

STALDER SHOOT: Giant swings in a straddle position with a piked body.

notes

Let Dr. Berg, the world's foremost authority on Jewish mysticism, open the door to your soul, show you how to *really* know yourself.

If *you* have started your journey into mysticism or have considered it, this book is recommended equipment for the *first* step.

With a simple, straightforward approach, Dr. Berg *de-mystifies* the Kabbalah and sheds light on the nature of man and his place in the universe.

Here is a unique synthesis of cosmic consciousness and the world of the five senses.

A living Kabbalist and the rarest of teachers, Dr. Berg presents an incredible simplification of the Kabbalah to the layman.

KABBALAH
FOR THE
LAYMAN

KABBALAH

FOR THE

LAYMAN

A GUIDE TO
COSMIC CONSCIOUSNESS

BY DR. PHILIP S. BERG

AN OPENING TO THE PORTALS OF
JEWISH MYSTICISM

Published by the Press of the Research Centre of Kabbalah
THE OLD CITY JERUSALEM, ISRAEL

ISBN Hard Cover 0–943–688–00–0
ISBN Soft Cover 0–943–688–01–9

Library of Congress Catalog Card Number TXU 94-666

First Printing, June 1982

Second Printing, November 1982

Third Printing, March 1983

Fourth Printing, March 1984

For further information address:
Research Centre of Kabbalah
P.O.Box 14168
The Old City, Jerusalem, Israel
or
Research Centre of Kabbalah
200 Park Ave. Suite 303E
New York, N.Y. 10017

BRANCHES IN ISRAEL
Tel Aviv, Safed, Haifa, Ber Sheva, Tikva Quarter, Neveh Zedek
Quarter, Rehovot

Printed in U. S. A. 1984

In memory
of
Robert J. Yohai

Rabbi Shimon Bar Yohai would say:
there are three crowns, the crown of
Torah, the crown of priesthood, and
the crown of royalty — but the crown
of a good name excels them all.
                              Pirke Avoth IV-17

ACKNOWLEDGMENT

I would like to express my grateful thanks for the help and advice given me by my wife, Karen, who patiently edited, criticized and typed the manuscript. Without her encouragement and faith, this book might have remained just another Leo dream.

TABLE OF CONTENTS

nothingness - channels of energy - constellation of the celestial regions-tree of life - the beginning.

PART THREE
MAKING THE CONNECTION
PRACTICAL APPLICATIONS

PREFACE

Eleven years ago, I received a strange phone call. A young lady was on the phone, inquiring in an excited tone of voice,
"Are you the Morrie Yohai who recently ordered a book from the Research Center of Kabbalah?"
"Yes, that's me", I replied.
"Are you related to Reb Shimon Bar Yohai?"
"How would I know? He lived almost two thousand years ago".
"Well, Rabbi Berg, the head of the Research Center would like to meet you. Can we arrange a meeting?"

To make a long and interesting story short, we had a meeting, the result was an arrangement to have me study Kabbalah with the Rabbi. This was something I had always wanted to do as I was interested in learning about the famous Jewish mystic whose name was also Yohai. There is a saying, "When you are ready to learn, your teacher will appear." This seemed to be happening.

We had many sessions of intense studying, or I should say learning together, as the Rabbi always referred to our "learning" sessions since he expected them to be mutual experiences. During one of these, I asked him why there were so few books out in English that did a creditable job of explaining the esoteric concepts we were covering. He pointed out that most of the books were not written by kabbalists, therefore lacked the true essence of kabbalistic thought. He said that one of these days he would write one for interested people — a primer for the layman. However, at the present time he was busy editing and putting out books of source material, books by Hyim Vital, Moses Luzzato, Rabbi Ashlag and the like.

That was eleven years ago. In the intervening years Dr. Berg has published many books in English and Hebrew of source material. He has gone to Israel and set up schools where courses in different aspects of Kabbalah are studied — schools in Tel Aviv, Jerusalem, Haifa and Beer-Sheva. While in Israel, he finally put down his own thoughts in regard to offering a meaningful introduction to Kabbalah. This book, *Kabbalah for the Layman,* is the result.

So, if you are ready to learn, your teacher has appeared.

Morrie R. Yohai
18 January 1981
13 Shevat 5741
President

A NOTE TO THE READER

It is of the utmost importance that the reader strive for a clear understanding and comprehension of the basic concepts and terminology of Kabbalah to provide a firm basis for more advanced studies. The reader is urged to read carefully the section on "Main Teachings" (Chapter VIII); without it the terms and concepts used in the text may be misleading. An inclusive glossary has also been provided at the back of the book for further guidance.

It may seem, on occasion, as though definitions and explanations are repeated, but successive readings of the book will reveal increasingly profound levels of meaning as the essential unity of the teachings of Kabbalah becomes apparent.

INTRODUCTION

For a long time the Kabbalah has remained virtually inaccessible to the average Jew: its study has been restricted either to the more Orthodox sects of Judaism or to academic scholars, neither of whom have felt the need to strive for a wider appreciation and understanding of the teachings of the Kabbalists. Orthodox Judaism has always stressed the prime importance of Talmudic studies, regarding Kabbalah as suitable only for those who are already knowledgeable in Talmud and Mishnah, and who have reached an age when they can cope with the secrets of esoteric wisdom. The academic world, on the other hand, evidently sees in Kabbalah the ideal field for research, complete with abstruse texts, colourful personalities and masses of symbolism and allusion to be collected, collated and set down in numerous learned papers. Here, too, there is no recognisable attempt to treat the vast literature of Kabbalah as a living and viable system of thought, and few attempts have been made to present the material gleaned from research in a form that could be understood by the vast majority of Jews who lack any sort of specialised knowledge in the field. The ordinary Jew who wants to find out more about the nature and content of the study of Kabbalah will, therefore, find himself set about with difficulties: if he approaches "religious figures", he will inevitably be dissuaded — either through the widespread ignorance that exists even within Orthodox circles about Kabbalah, or by the stringency of the qualifications that will be demanded before he can undertake even preliminary investigations. The result of this neglect of Kabbalah — which, as we shall see, signifies a lack of understanding of the central position held by Kabbalah in understanding the Torah —can be seen in the all-too-frequent degeneration of Judaism into a marginal social activity, and in the flight of young people away from Judaism to the more mystically-inclined eastern religions.

The purpose of this book, therefore, is not just to provide the reader with a taste of the vast world of Jewish mystical thought, and an experience of how Kabbalah can be brought to bear on the problems facing the world today, but to argue the appropriateness and necessity of returning to the understanding of the universe and its law that is provided for us by the Kabbalah.

There can be no doubt that the recent rebirth of interest in mysticism and the occult among the young has given an important impetus to the resurgence of Kabbalah as a living force in Jewish studies: it has come as a surprise and a revelation to many to discover within Judaism the unsuspected existence of such a fully-fledged, complex and absorbing system as Kabbalah — a system, furthermore, that can deal confidently with all the problems thrown up by existence in the twentieth century, an area in which traditional authorities have all too often been seen to flounder. Judaism is frequently experienced by young people as an arbitrary and archaic system of coercive and restrictive rules designed to enable a mythical nation of ex-slaves to survive for forty years in a desert, and subsequently fossilized through the minute arrangements of the sages until the result would seem of more interest to the historian and the archaeologist than to the person facing the problems of finding out what it means to be a Jew in modern society.

How refreshing, then, to discover the Kabbalah: here we find that all forms of coercion are finally ruled out. It is pointed out that the Almighty, who created each and every one of us, does not force us to do good. How then, can we justify the use of force and threats to compel one another to certain forms of behaviour. According to the Kabbalah, no precept should be fulfilled merely in the name of Tradition or Commemoration, without a deeper understanding of the reasons, underlying that precept; the only reason for observance is that, using the understanding of Kabbalah together with the tools and instruments provided for our use by the Torah, one can reconstruct the mystical dimension of a time lost in the past, a time whose mystical energies continue to exist in the universe. These meta-physical energies, which the Kabbalah describes in minute detail, are available for our use each and every day, provided we know how to draw them down and to what use we can put them. Rabbi Shimon bar Yohai, the author of the Zohar (the Book of Splendour, the classic work on the hidden understanding of the Torah) made exactly this point in his refutation of the viewpoint that religious obligation was a sufficient reason for ritual and the fulfilling of mitzvot (precepts): "Prayer and ritual, devoid of meaning and spirituality, are like straw — the epitome of life-lessness."[1] If religion is not seen as a moving force in our society, the cause may therefore lie in its current inability to meet the growing spiritual needs of its members.

Closer to our own time we have the observation of Rabbi Yehuda Ashlag (1886-1955), who translated the Zohar and its concepts from the original Aramaic into modern Hebrew: "If these needs are not met, then we may expect a totally despiritua-lised and demoralised society, the likes of which has never been experienced in the history of mankind."[2]

It is becoming increasingly clear that what is needed is a genuine moral and spiritual system that will both enable us to redefine such basic terms as Good and Evil for a generation to whom they have become meaningless, and help us make sense of a universe that now contains space travel, drug addiction, atomic destruction, television and the laser. It is the contention of this book that knowledge of Kabbalah leads one to a correct appreciation of the significance of these problems, and provides the key to their understanding and eventual mastery.

The widespread ignorance surrounding the nature and con-tent of Kabbalah has led to the growth of false ideas, fear and mistrust; those few Kabbalists in the past who misused their powers, or misinterpreted their role as the bearers of wisdom, have had a detrimental effect on the popular attitute towards Kabbalah that is quite disproportionate to their numbers. In the absence of arguments to the contrary from either the Orthodox community or the academics, it is generally believed that the study of Kabbalah is an unnecessary and dangerous pursuit. It is deemed unneccesary because all that a Jew needs to know is contained within the Torah and the commentaries, and dangerous in that it threatens not only the balance and sanity of the individual, but also the well-being of the community at large. In fact, it was precisely for this reason that Rabbi Shimon bar Yohai made the vital distinction between *Ta'amei Torah* (the hidden understanding of Torah that is accessible to all who wish to learn) and *Sitrei Torah* (the secret teachings that are kept hidden for those who have reached the point where they can deal adequately with the power contained therein). While the aspects of Sitrei Torah are concealed by various means from the sight and understanding of all but a few, the insights of Ta'amei Torah are for the benefit of all Jews, regardless of age or sect: indeed, Rabbi Shimon went so far as to claim that the teachings of Ta'amei Torah could benefit even a child of six.[3]

However, the fact that some areas of Kabbalah do contain revelations of the nature and structure of the universe that bring with them an increase in the understanding and power of the individual is not, in itself, a sufficient reason for the neglect of the study of Kabbalah that we have witnessed in recent years. On the contrary, it would seem that any system of belief that claims viability and importance in the twentieth century must contain a large — and, therefore, potentially dangerous — aspect of power. A moment's reflection will show that contemporary Judaism is faced with two choices: it can either continue on its present path, commemorating in its daily life the history of its ancestors, dwindling year by year in both numbers and influence, or it can reveal its importance and power in the world today, demonstrating that it alone has the power to re-unify the fragmented and scattered peoples of the earth. The diversity that we see all around us, and which distracts us from the central unity of all existence, is like the differences to be found in the branches and twigs of a tree. The overwhelming need today is for a unifying force to counteract this diversity, to enable people to see their part in the unrolling drama — a knowledge of the structure and the power of the root of all things, which is to be found *only* in the Kabbalah.

Rabbi Shimon indicated that, in response to the crises of a particular age, spiritual meaning and purpose will transcend organisation and schismatic rivalries. By this he meant that involvement in matters of true spirituality takes people away from petty factionalism and allows unity of purpose to emerge. This goal of spiritual and communal unity is best realised by a clear exposition of Judaism itself, an exposition that is best achieved through the study of Kabbalah.[4]

An excellent, if unfortunate, example of the widespread malaise that now affects Judaism is the deep division over the issue of *Halacha*. Each faction has its own approach and understanding on the subject, and discussions between factions seem to be limited to the spirited defense of particular positions. An obvious and desirable alternative would be to develop an approach to Halacha that brings out its deeper and unifying dimensions, stressing the experience of the spirituality of Halacha, and not just its ritualised performance: this becomes possible through an understanding of Ta'amei Torah, the reasons for Torah that are expounded in the Zohar. No longer need the Jew resort to apologetics and obscurantism when faced with criticism. The Kabbalah has revealed that science, for so long held to be a refutation of religion, is nothing more than a commentary on the Torah, and that the apparently random and meaningless rules and rituals of Halacha are, in fact, expressions of basic laws of the universe, no more arbitrary than the laws of thermodynamics or chemical formulae. The traditional justification of "kah katuv" — thus it is written — is no longer needed, for it implies that there is no greater reason for carrying out a precept than that we are told to do so, this despite the fact that the sages of the Talmud were clearly not prepared to take anything on face value, and argued strenuously over the meaning of every word of the Torah. In the years to come, with the increasing knowledge and understanding of Kabbalah, we shall witness the very scientists who claimed to have dispensed with the need for religion and belief turning to the teachings of the Zohar to find knowledge of the essential structure and laws of the universe. Then Halacha will be seen in its true light — not the convenient focus for factionalism it is today, but the expression of the underlying movement and flow of the cosmos.

PART ONE

ORIGINS AND HISTORY OF KABBALAH

R. Hiya adduced here the verse: "I was asleep but my heart waked, it is the voice of my beloved that knocketh", the Holy One, blessed be He, saying, 'Open to me an opening no bigger than the eye of a needle, and I will open to thee the supernal gates'.

Zohar III, P. 95a.

CHAPTER 1

KABBALAH: A DEFINITION

From the foregoing discussion it should come as no surprise to learn that the definitions of Kabbalah are many and varied: for each academic writer Kabbalah will be seen as illuminating a different aspect of Jewish history, philosophy or religion. To the Orthodox Jew it might be another commentary on the Torah, albeit a rather exotic one; in less dedicated circles, Kabbalah has been seen as a form of clairvoyance, occultism or magic. To those of a mystical inclination, it appears as a key to immortality, the ultimate union of the soul with the Absolute, the Almighty. Yet all these definitions fall short of the real meaning of Kabbalah.

The literal meaning of the word Kabbalah is Receiving: thus, in the opening sentence of the Ethics of the Fathers, we read that "Moses received the Torah from Sinai" — the word used for "receive" being "kibel", the past tense of the verb "kabal". It was clear to the sages that the Torah received by Moses was unique in that it contained the knowledge necessary not only for the Jews of that time, but for all generations. Thus, when Rabbi Shimon came to reveal the mystical part of the Torah in the Zohar, he related it closely to the written Torah so as to demonstrate that Torah and Kabbalah are but different aspects of the same essential whole. The Torah itself represents the outer shell while Kabbalah is the inner core, concealed from sight — a relationship similar to that which exists between the physical body and soul. Torah reveals the word of G-d, while Kabbalah reveals the hidden and the revealed.

The very fact that the secrets of the universe are revealed

through the study of Receiving tells us a great deal about the nature of existence. We learn that the Desire to Receive is the basic mechanism by which the world operates, the dynamic process at the base of all physical and metaphysical manifestations. The title gives us a clue to this fundamental law, which is expounded in the body of Kabbalistic literature.

The Desire to Receive affects all creation because it is the basis of all creation: it affects all four levels of creation — human, animal, vegetative and inanimate. In an inanimate object the Desire to Receive is small; a rock or stone is almost independent of the physical world for its existence — it needs nothing to ensure its continuing existence; nonetheless, for it to exist at all it must contain some part of the Desire to Receive. As we move up the evolutionary scale, we find an increasing physical dependence upon the external world for survival culminating in Man, who has the greatest Desire to Receive of all Creation — not only for physical things, but also for intangible needs like peace, happiness and satisfaction. The culmination of the Desire to Receive is the Desire to Receive for others, which is equivalent to the Desire to Impart. We see this in its most sublime form in the celebration of the Sabbath, the high point of the Creation, which is the expression of G-d's Desire to Impart, and man's Desire to Receive. It is also at the root of the fundamental directive of the Holy Torah expressed by Rabbi Hillel in the words "Love your neighbour as yourself." Only when the Desire to Receive is transformed into the Desire to Impart to others is it completed — loving your neighbour, you are also, in the profoundest sense, loving yourself and, ultimately, your Creator.

The sublime teachings of Jewish mysticism are also called "The Wisdom of Kabbalah" and "The Wisdom of the Truth". The root meaning of the word 'wisdom' as it is used here is alluded to by the sages[6] when they ask, "who is wise?" and reply, "He who sees consequences of actions." As soon as he observes an action the wise man perceives what will be born and result from it; he is like a good doctor who can detect the symptoms of a disease at an early stage, and then knows the course that disease will run, and its eventual outcome. Indeed, the mark of a wise man in any trade or profession is that he does not have to wait for the future to know what the future has in store: the knowledge that he possesses is of the root, from which all subsequent actions can be known. Kabbalah, then, may be understood as the study of wisdom: it allows the individual to understand the true meaning of the Creation, which is the root of all existence — not only on the physical, but also on the metaphysical level. By revealing the root of Creation, it enables us to unravel the mysteries of the working of the universe and shows us the potential consequences of all possible actions.

Yet one should not forget that mysticism is rendered in Hebrew as *hochmot hanistar*, the wisdom of the unexplained, or of the unknown: for all that the Kabbalah freely offers us knowledge of the original causes of all things, we should always remember that this is only a part of its wisdom. Rabbi Ashlag, by translating and providing commentaries to the classical works of Kabbalah, has stripped away much of the mystique surrounding Ta'amei Torah, so that it can be studied with profit by all who wish; Sitrei Torah, the concealed sections of Kabbalah, are still — and will always remain — hidden from those who might misunderstand or misuse the knowledge contained therein.

CHAPTER 2

THE ORIGINS OF KABBALAH

The first known printed work on Jewish mysticism is the Sefer Yetzirah, whose authorship has been attributed to the Patriarch Abraham. Containing ideas and concepts of the most sublime and elevated level, this text has not been used by Kabbalists of the past due to the difficulty of defining exactly the terms and hidden meanings it contains. The most elaborate and lengthy work to have appeared in Jewish esoteric studies is the Zohar. Those who have studied it and understood fully the significance of its teachings are unanimous in ascribing it to the saintly sage of the Mishnaic period, Rabbi Shimon Bar Yohai. The authorship of the Zohar is a subject of debate among those who study Kabbalah as an academic pastime, without ever attempting to understand the content of the works they analyse. Many of these scholars maintain that the Zohar was written by the 11th century Kabbalist, Moses de Leon, of blessed memory, or by others among his contemporaries. When the holy Zohar is better understood, however, it becomes evident that only someone of the stature and spirituality of Rabbi Shimon could have composed the work.

We know that each generation of Jews has a lesser understanding of Torah than its predecessor.[7] To credit a book such as the Zohar to any age other than that of the Tanna'im, the compilers of the Mishnah who lived from the first to the third centuries C.E., is simply not possible, since this would imply that the level of spiritual consciousness and understanding of Moses de Leon was comparable to, if not higher than that of the saintly Tanna'im. When the historians elect Moses de Leon as author of

the Zohar, they thereby neglect the opinion of such great Kabbalists as Moses Cordovero, Shlomo Alkabetz, Joseph Caro,
Isaac Luria, Moses Luzzato and many others — men for whom
the Zohar was a way of life, rather than a field of study, and who
were unanimous in there agreement that Rabbi Shimon was the
author of the Zohar. The underlying assumption of these great
men was that the man who wrote the Zohar must have been on
the same level of spirituality as its contents, and that only Rabbi
Shimon fitted that description.

Let us now, therefore, look at the history of this great sage in
an attempt to understand the verdict of the famous Kabbalists
mentioned above.

When Israel was under the rule of Rome Rabbi Shimon was a
disciple of Rabbi Akiva, who continued to teach Torah despite
the Roman decree forbidding its study. Rabbi Akiva was captured
and put to death, whereupon Rabbi Shimon launched a verbal
attack on the Romans, accusing them of intolerance and cruelty,
and was himself sentenced to death as a result. He fled with his
son Elazar to a cave in the mountains near the Galilee town of
Pequin, where he hid in a cave for thirteen years until the
Emperor's death made it safe for them to leave.

As to the revelation of the holy Zohar, the sages of blessed
memory[8], relate the following legend. The thirteen years that
Rabbi Shimon and his son spent in the cave marked a turning
point in the history of the great body of Jewish esoteric knowledge. In the seclusion of the cave Rabbi Shimon was visited twice
a day by the prophet Elijah, who revealed to him the secrets of
the Zohar. The deeper and more comprehensive sections, known
as the Ra'ya Mehemna, are a record of the discourses that also
took place between Rabbi Shimon and Moses himself, the
beloved shepherd of the title.

One should not take this to mean that the secrets of the Zohar
were revealed only to Rabbi Shimon. His teacher, Rabbi Akiva,
and several others before him were fully versed in all the teachings of the Zohar. In fact, the entire understanding of Kabbalah

was presented in its oral form to Israel on Mount Sinai; many studied and understood the dazzling truths of Jewish mysticism, but few could make others see and understand. For this, the written text of the Zohar, Jewry would have to wait for Pequin and Rabbi Shimon.

The question still remains, however, of why Rabbi Shimon was chosen to set down the teachings of the Zohar in preference to his teacher, Rabbi Akiva, or indeed any of the other giants of the Kabbalah who preceded him. This problem has been the source of many commentaries and parables; it is often stressed, for instance, that through his fugitive and solitary life, Rabbi Shimon was able to overcome the physical restraints and limitations that normally prevent the attainment of the higher levels of spiritual consciousness. He was thus able to transcend the laws governing time and space, thereby acquiring root knowledge of all existence as we experience it on this earthly plane. Thus we find in the Zohar not only discussions of strictly spiritual matters but also fundamental concepts in such fields as medicine, astrology, law, telecommunications and psychiatry. But the problem still remains — why was Rabbi Shimon chosen to live in a cave for thirteen years? The answer is to be found in a more basic problem that relates to the spiritual history of the Jewish people.

Within the physical body of Man we find two distinct motivating factors called the Inner Light and the Encircling Light. The Inner Light is the element of light contained within man upon his descent into this mundane world at birth. The Encircling Light is the element of light which the individual merits during his lifetime through good deeds and actions — in other words, it is acquired gradually and is not present at birth. The difference between the two Lights is determined by the degree to which an individual is able to subordinate the physical body to the Light; in effect, the Inner Light that accompanies man is merely an aid in the pursuit of spiritual ascent. The degree to which an individual is limited by the constraints of time, space and motion — the physical laws of the universe — is dependent on the degree to which he manages to control the Desire to Receive of his body, or the evil inclination. Gradually, man acquires the Encircling Light and ascends the ladder of spirituality.

The Ari (Rabbi Isaac Luria), explaining the inner makeup of Moses, states that "Moses encompassed the Inner and Encircling Lights; the inclusion of the Inner Light is alluded to by the verse 'and she saw he was good' (Exodus 2:2), and the Encircling Light is denoted by the verse 'the skin of his face shone' (Exodus 34:30)[9]. These two qualities were required before Moses could have received the entire Torah including, as I have said, the understanding of Kabbalah and the explanations of its esoteric meanings.

We learn that Rabbi Shimon was a reincarnation of Moses himself[10], in reference to which the Zohar says, "The son of Yohai (meaning Rabbi Shimon) knows how to observe his ways; if he ventures into the deep sea, he looks all round before entering, in order to establish how he will accomplish the task in one attempt."[11] From this statement the Ari draws the following conclusions: "One must understand that among the souls of the righteous, there are those who possess the Encircling Light, and who have the capability of communicating the esoteric mysteries of the Torah by means of concealment and cryptic references, so as to prevent those who lack merit from understanding it. Rabbi Shimon's soul incorporated the Encircling Light from birth; he thus had the power to clothe the esoteric lore and also to discourse on it. Subsequently, permission was granted to Rabbi Shimon to write the book of Splendour: the sanction to write this book of wisdom was not given to the sages who preceded Rabbi Shimon because, even though they were highly knowledgeable in this wisdom, even to the extent of exceeding Rabbi Shimon, they lacked his ability to clothe and protect the esoteric lore. This is the meaning of the reference to Rabbi Shimon made above."[12]

CHAPTER III:

RABBI SHIMON BAR YOHAI AND THE GREATER ASSEMBLY

A convenient and valuable method of studying the historical development of Kabbalah is to examine the lives and personalities of the exceptional individuals who were chosen to disseminate its teachings. Among these men the foremost group was that of Rabbi Shimon and his followers.

It is told that when Rabbi Shimon emerged from the cave in which he and his son Elazar had spent thirteen years learning the secrets of Kabbalah, his body was covered with sores: his father-in-law, Rabbi Pinhas, wept bitterly when he saw the state of Rabbi Shimon's body, saying, "How bitter it is for me to see you in such a state!" Whereupon Rabbi Shimon replied, "I am happy that you see me like this — otherwise I would not be what I am."[13] Clearly he regarded his physical condition and discomfort as unimportant — even necessary for him to have reached the spiritual heights that he had attained.

Rabbi Shimon went on to select eight disciples,[14] who, together with himself and his son, formed the 'Great Assembly'.[15] They chose a spot on the road from Meron to Safed in Galilee and began to discuss the hidden meanings and mysteries of Torah that had been revealed to their teacher. Rabbi Shimon taught his disciples both Sitrei Torah and Ta'amei Torah. He revealed the Divine secrets, going back to the period before even the primal vessels had been formed. It was necessary for him to transmit ideas-even if they were sometimes unintelligible to his audience — so that they would not be lost to future generations.

Before the Assembly was disbanded, however, three of the

disciples — Rabbi Yosi ben Jacob, Rabbi Hezekiah and Rabbi Yisa — died. They had absorbed as much spiritual light as their capacity allowed and had thus moved beyond the physical sphere. Those students who were left saw the three being carried away by angels.

Rabbi Shimon wept and said, "Is it possible that we are being punished for revealing that which has been hidden since Moses stood on Mount Sinai?"[16] At that moment a voice exclaimed from above, "Praiseworthy are you, Shimon bar Yohai, praiseworthy is your portion and the portion of your assembly. Through you was revealed that which was not even revealed to the upper Celestial Hosts. Therefore, praiseworthy is your portion: your three students departed because their lives were fulfilled."

The light that emanated from Rabbi Shimon was of such intensity that it was said to resemble the reality that will exist at the end of the period of correction (G'mar haTikun), the period in which we now live, when we enter the Age of the Messiah.[17] The vessels of the three students came from the lower spheres and consequently could not contain or endure the light that had entered them, just as ordinary glass cannot withstand boiling water.

Such, was the power of the author of the Zohar, a man who had truly transcended the limitations of time, space and motion.

One day Rabbi Shimon observed that the world was covered by darkness and that the Light was concealed. His son, Rabbi Elazar, said to him, "Let us try to find out what the Creator means to accomplish."

They found an angel who appeared to them in the form of a great mountain, spewing forth thirty torches of fire, and Rabbi Shimon asked him what he intended to do. "I am instructed to destroy the world," replied the angel, "because mankind does not contain in its midst thirty righteous individuals."

Rabbi Shimon said to the Angel, "Go before the Creator, and

tell him that Bar Yohai is among the inhabitants of the world, and his merit is equal to that of thirty righteous men."

The angel ascended to the Creator and exclaimed, "Lord of the universe, are You aware of Bar Yohai's words to me?" Whereupon the Creator replied,

"Descend and destroy the world as you were commanded: take no notice of Bar Yohai!"

Seeing the angel reappear, Rabbi Shimon told him, "If you do not ascend again to the Almighty with my request, I shall prevent you from ever reaching the heavens again: and this time, when you come before the Creator repeat to Him that if the world lacks thirty righteous men, He should spare it for the sake of ten; if there are not ten such men to be found in the whole world, then ask Him to spare mankind for the sake of two men, my son and I; and if you deem these two insufficient, then preserve the world for the sake of one man and I am that one. For it is written, 'But the righteous is an everlasting foundation (Proverbs 10:25).

At that very moment a voice from Heaven was heard, saying, "Praiseworthy is your portion, Shimon Bar Yohai, for the Lord above issues a decree, and you seek to countermand it; surely for you is written the verse: He will fulfill the desire of those that fear Him!" (Psalms 145:19).[18]

Here we see Rabbi Shimon, through the power of his Inner and Encircling Light, going so far as to challenge the authority of the Creator. So firmly did he believe in the justice of his cause. But his power was not only used in this way, to ward off the encroaching darkness! he struggled throughout his life to introduce Light into places where ignorance and superstition reigned, to make the metaphysical as well as the physical world comprehensible, and to link all the levels of existence to reveal a world of true beauty and harmony.

So pure and righteous was the soul of Rabbi Shimon that the Angel of Death could never utter his name. When the Angel of Death appeared before the Creator demanding the death of an individual, he would cite the evil deeds which necessitated the death penalty. When it came to Rabbi Shimon, however, he could find no evil deeds to hold against him.[19] Then one day the *Yetzer Hara* (the Evil Inclination) appeared before the Creator and demanded that He immediately recall Rabbi Shimon from his earthly abode to his rightful place in the Garden of Eden. This was a strange request, a departure from the normal procedure; the Evil Inclination usually demands the recall of an individual for the express purpose of imposing justice, punishment, or even death. But the plea of the Evil Inclination for the recall of Rabbi Shimon went as follows:

"My purpose in the physical world is to divert the individual from a humane and righteous path to one of wrongdoing: but I have never before encountered a man like Rabbi Shimon bar Yohai. Not only have I been unsuccessful in my attempts to divert him from the proper course of piety and righteousness, but he has actually sought me out that he might be confronted with temptation, in order to turn this temptation to some useful and fruitful purpose. You must remove him from the world: I have nowhere to conceal myself from him and I fear that my objective in this physical world will fail."[20]

For this reason alone, Rabbi Shimon was summoned to the Garden of Eden. The day of his death, known as the Smaller or Lesser Assembly, was no ordinary day: "On the day that Rabbi Shimon *desired* to leave this world, he prepared his final words. To all his friends gathered beside him, he revealed new esoteric mysteries. Rabbi Abba wrote, 'The Light was so great that I could not approach him. When the Light departed, I saw that the Holy Light (Rabbi Shimon) had left this world. His son, Rabbi Elazar, took his father's hands and kissed them saying, 'My father, my father — there were three, and only one is now left.' (The reference is to Rabbi Shimon, his father-in-law Rabbi Pinchas, and Rabbi Elazar.)

"The peoples of the surrounding communities assembled, each demanding that the Rabbi be buried in their midst; then the bed upon which the body lay rose up and flew through the air, preceded by a torch of fire, until it reached the cave at Meron. Here it descended, and everyone knew that Rabbi Shimon had reached his final resting place. All this took place on the thirty-third day of the Omer, which is the eighteenth day of the month of Iyyar."[21]

To this very day, tens of thousands of pilgrims make the journey to Meron to pay tribute to Rabbi Shimon. Others come in the hope of finding an answer to their prayers, and fulfilment of their needs, through the influence of ha Or haKodesh, the Holy Light, Rabbi Shimon bar Yohai.

CHAPTER IV

GOLDEN AGE OF SAFED

In the year 1492 of the present era, a tragedy for the Jewish people was enacted in Spain, when Queen Isabella and King Ferdinand issued a decree of expulsion that sealed the fate of the Jews in that country. Within four months, all those Jews who refused to renounce their faith would be compelled to leave Spain. A great centre of Jewish learning, one which had profoundly influenced Jewish thought and expression, was in ruins.

In the wake of this spiritual and physical upheaval, many Jews migrated to the Middle East. A number of them settled in the Upper Galilee, drawn to the ancient town of Safed; here a group of Jewish mystics were setting the stage for the numerous mystical movements of the next four hundred years, among them being the resurgence of interest in the study of Kabbalah.

From a practical viewpoint, one may attribute the sudden popularity of Kabbalah directly to the misfortunes that overtook the Jews in Spain. Their 'Golden Age' having been forcibly brought to a close and their future uncertain, they sought to understand the reasons for their suffering. The philosophical teachings of the day were not sufficient to explain away the overwhelming burdens that had been suddenly thrust upon them, and they came to view Kabbalah as a means of clarifying and solving the puzzling complexities of existence.

This great convergence of mystically-oriented people on Safed was by no means a coincidence. They were re-enacting a scene that had taken place some fifteen hundred years earlier. The date of the expulsion from Spain, the ninth day of Av, was also the date of the destruction of the First and Second Temples; shortly after the destruction of the Second Temple in 70 C.E., Rabbi Shimon had revealed the Zohar. Fifteen centuries later, following the destruction of the Sephardic community in Spain, the practical application of this esoteric wisdom would become an integral part of Jewish tradition and learning. The great spiritual personalities of the time had returned to their source, their place of origin, the Land of Israel.

The historical interpretation of the events of this period merely serves to demonstrate the inadequacy of a methodology based on superficial actions. To dismiss the rebirth of Kabbalah in Safed as nothing more than the product of the expulsion from Spain and subsequent Messianic hope centering in the Holy Land is to ignore the real significance of what happened. Cause and effect, as the raw materials of the historian, are of only limited use, since they are only obvious when bound together closely by time. No reputable historian is going to risk his reputation on the association of two sequences of events that took place fifteen centuries apart, yet this is where the truth lies. The coming together of so many spiritual individuals was unparalleled in an age when the oppression of Jewish communities was widespread, but it was only the Spanish Jews who moved in numbers to Israel.

It is certainly true that the idea of the Messiah was closely linked to this migration, but in a radical sense that did not include the imminent arrival of the Messiah among its aims or expectations. It was, rather, the realisation stemming from the words of the Kabbalah, that the redemption of the Jewish people and of mankind as a whole was deeply linked with the land of Israel. In Isaiah's prophetic vision of the future, he states: "For out of Zion shall go forth the Law, and the word of the Lord from Jerusalem."[22] "There is an apparent contradiction here, since the Israelites had already received the Law from Mount Sinai, which was not within the boundaries of Israel; nor did the Law go forth from Zion or Jerusalem. What, then, did the Prophet Isaiah mean by this passage?

The Zohar compares the Pentateuch, the Five Books of the Law, to the body of man, and the Kabbalah to his soul; thus the 'body' of the law was given on Mount Sinai, but the inner meaning, the 'soul' of the Torah in its written form, would wait to be revealed from the Land of Israel. This revelation is the instrument by which Israel and the rest of the world will finally be redeemed, realising the dream of "peace on earth, good will to all men." Thus the migration to Israel can be seen as part of the Divine plan, the next step on the road to redemption. The great minds of mysticism were to gather in Safed to prepare the necessary texts that would, in time, enable the Jewish community as a whole to comprehend the soul of Torah — the Kabbalah.

In Safed the Jews of Spain and nearby Provence lived a simple, religious life, seeking only peace and piety. With Rabbi Shimon's interpretation of the true meaning of Torah as their foundation, Kabbalah flourished as never before. This influence was most strongly felt in the schools of Rabbi Moses Cordovero and Rabbi Isaac Luria, two of the most important centres of study in 16th century Safed. As the Sephardic community spread out, the study of Kabbalah extended to Italy and Turkey. In Salonika, then part of Turkey, Solomon Alkabetz (1505-1584), the composer of the Sabbath hymn "Lecha Dodi" (Come, My Beloved) established a centre for the teaching of Kabbalah; shortly afterwards, he, too, was drawn to Safed, to take part in the great revitalization of the Torah then taking place there.

The Kabbalists of Safed made a conscious effort to preserve the entire Torah, with its fundamental principles and laws, by extending it so that its relevance to all aspects of life could be seen. Evolving from the structure of traditional Rabbinic Judaism, it strove to present a religious experience that would provide its adherents with sufficient energy to meet the demands of daily life. Many of the pratices of Judaism — such as the three festivals of pilgrimage,[23] the religious laws and rituals relating to an agrarian lifestyle[24] had become obsolete for the Jews of Israel and the Diaspora following the destruction of the Second Temple. The survival of Judaism as a living religious system depended on the ability of the Torah to improve the lives of Jews from many different cultural backgrounds.

Rabbi Moses Cordovero was drawn 'as by a thirst' to the wisdom of Kabbalah in 1522; he studied in Safed with Rabbi Solomon Alkabetz, whose sister he married. He proved a gifted teacher and writer, composing the first comprehensive commentary on the Zohar ("Or Yakar", the Exalted Light). The manuscript, obtained on microfilm from the Vatican Library, has already yielded many volumes of priceless teachings. His other major works include "Or Nerav", "Shiur Koma", "Tomer Deborah", and "Pardes Remonim".

Rabbi Isaac Luria, the Ari Hakodesh (Holy Lion), was born in Jerusalem in 1534. According to legend the Prophet Elijah appeared at his circumcision ceremony to act as Sandak (godfather), and told his father to take great care of the child, for he would be the source of an exalted light. After the death of his father, his mother, who was of Sephardic descent, took him to the home of her brother Mordechai Francis, a wealthy and respected man in the Jewish community of Cairo. In Egypt, he studied with the famous Rabbis Bezalel and David Zimra (the Radbaz). At the age of seventeen he married one of his cousins.

The Ari was a Talmudic authority before he had reached the age of twenty, and soon mastered all the material his mentors had to offer him. He then discovered the Zohar, and lived as a hermit in a remote place by the Nile for thirteen years, while he studied the secrets of the Kabbalah. In 1569 he settled in Safed, where he studied with Moses Cordovero until he became a master in his own right, with a circle of devoted disciples.

The Ari developed a new system for understanding the mysteries of the Zohar: called the Lurianic method, it focuses on the Ten Sefirot or Luminous Emanations, and sheds new light on the hidden wisdom of the Kabbalah. His complete understanding of the mysteries of the Zohar, together with the other great powers that he manifested during his lifetime, were a result of his unique spiritual identity. His student, Haim Vital, tells the following story:

"One day I went with my teacher (the Ari) to the site where Rabbi Shimon and his disciples had assembled and created the Greater Assembly. On the eastern side of the path was a stone containing two large fissures; the northern fissure was where Rabbi Shimon had sat, and the southern one where Rabbi Abba had sat. At a nearby tree, facing these two clefts, Rabbi Elazar had been seated. The Ari seated himself within the nothern fissure, as Rabbi Shimon had done before him, and I sat within the southern one, not knowing that this was the seat of Rabbi Abba. It was only after this encounter that my teacher explained to me the significance of what had taken place. Now I know what he had in mind when he told me that I contain the spark of one of the members of the Idra (assembly)."[25]

Anyone familiar with the writings of the Ari will realise that his clarity and depth of thought and understanding could only come from one blessed with the spirit of Rabbi Shimon: only Rabbi Shimon's soul would have been capable of the feats of transcendence that are clearly indicated in the Ari's writings.

Some people thought that the Ari was the harbinger of the Messianic Age, and extraordinary legend grew up concerning his piety and righteousness. One Erev Shabbat (Sabbath eve) the Ari assembled his disciples and declared that he could effect the coming of the Messiah that very Shabbat. He stressed to all present the importance of complete harmony, warning them to be aware of the slightest confrontation with one another. So the unique Shabbat began, and all went well throughout Friday night and Shabbat morning. Towards the close of Shabbat, a trivial argument broke out among the children of the Ari's disciples. This quarrel escalated until the parents intervened, leading in turn to a disagreement among two of the disciples. Shabbat ended without the appearance of the Messiah; the disciples showed their disappointment at being unworthy of his coming, and asked their teacher the reason for this. The Ari replied sadly,

"For a small pittance, the arrival of the Messiah was forestalled." Little did his disciples know that Satan resorts to any means to divert men from their noble intentions; knowing all too well the disciples' awareness of the important task of maintaining harmony among themselves, he chose a covert and unsuspected approach to gain his objective of disunity. "Thus," concluded the Ari "the coming of the Messiah does not mean that we must wait for some individual to ride through the Gate of Mercy in the Eastern Wall of the city of Jerusalem, mounted on a white donkey. Rather, the presence of goodwill towards men and peace on earth, as indicated in the verse "The wolf shall dwell with the lamb, the leopard shall lie down with the kid (Isaiah 11:6) is the Messiah. The Messiah is nothing more than the symbol of world harmony." Hearing this, the disciples departed with bowed heads.

On another occasion the Ari gathered his disciples together for a journey to Jerusalem in order to spend Shabbat there. When they heard his intention they were overcome with bewilderment and asked their teacher how he could contemplate such a long journey when the arrival of the Shabbat was only a matter of minutes away. Smiling, the Ari replied, "The elements of time, space and motion are merely an expression of the limitations imposed by the physical body on the soul. When the soul has sway over the body, however, these limiting factors cease to exist. Let us now proceed to Jerusalem, therefore, for our corporeal bodies have lost their influence over our souls." In this way, singing mystical chants, the Ari and his disciples arrived in Jerusalem in time to celebrate the coming of the Sabbath.

At the age of thirty-eight, on the fifth day of Av 1572, the Ari completed his task on earth and ascended to the place waiting for him in the Garden of Eden. To his most trusted and favoured pupil Haim Vital, and to Haim's son, Shmuel Vital, he gave the task of recording his thoughts and teachings on paper as a record for posterity of the Golden Age of Kabbalah in Safed. These two devoted followers summarized, as far as was possible, the deeds and wisdom of their teacher, producing the volumes that we now regard as the Ari's writings; Haim Vital became a legendary figure and a source of wisdom for later Kabbalists, who could now refer to a concise and clear literary work that laid open the hithertofore obscure and abstruse contents of the central work of Kabbalistic literature, the Zohar.

The faculty of human reason has alienated many people from the basic tenets of the Torah, due largely to the difficulty in accepting as intrinsic truths those teachings that are based on a literal understanding of the Law. A prime objective of the Ari's commentary was that truth should be presented in a logical, consecutive manner. The system devised by Rabbi Shimon was not immediately apparent to students and scholars of the Kabbalah, leading some to claim that the knowledge of the Book of Splendour was irrational and illogical. The writings of the Ari, however, refute this claim completely, in as much as they represent a commentary on the Zohar that can be both grasped by the intellect and perceived by the senses. Where ambiguous and figurative expressions and seemingly inconsequential stories in the Torah leave an impression of irrelevancy, the writings caution the reader to beware of literal interpretations. Where some aspect of Torah appears to contradict common sense, the Ari reminds us that the metaphors of the law were originally intended merely to enable the uneducated to comprehend to the best of their abilities. To the knowledgeable a deeper interpretation of such stories should present itself. The parables themselves are of no great value until their inner, sublime meanings have been made intelligible by means of the study of the Kabbalah.

We have already seen that the "accidents" of history that brought together the great minds of Kabbalah in Safed, were, in fact, part of the eternal scheme leading to the eventual redemption of mankind. The presence of Haim and Shmuel Vital was a part of this unfolding, and is demonstrated by their unerring grasp of an enormous body of sublime Kabbalistic scholarship. They presented concepts that were not perceptible through the five senses and identified truths that could not be attained through the exercise of logic or imagination. The Ari himself implied that his reincarnation on this earth was largely for the purpose of instructing Haim Vital in the mysteries of Kabbalah. Furthermore, his presence permitted Vital to rectify faults in the many reincarnated personalities that he contained — among them being Cain, Korach, Yohanan ben Zakai and Rabbi Akiva.[26] In addition, the Ari told Vital that his soul contained sparks of the Divine Essence that were of a higher degree than those possessed by many of the supernal angels. "But more than that I may not reveal; if I were to reveal your essence to you, you would quite literally fly with joy, but I have not been granted permission to discuss your incarnation in greater detail."[27]

One Friday night Moses Alshikh — the most important homiletician of the 16th century — came to the Ari and asked him why he should receive the Ari's teachings only through Haim Vital, who was considerably his junior; the Ari replied, "I have returned to this world solely for the purpose of teaching Haim Vital, since no other student is capable of learning so much as a single letter from me."[28] When Vital himself put the same question to him, the Ari told him that the study of Kabbalah did not depend on the student's level of understanding, intelligence or active intellect, but rather on his spirit which is incarnated from a supernal level.[29] He told Vital that he would soon come face to face with the Prophet Elijah and talk of many things with him; also, through repentance and good deeds, that he would complete and amend his *Nefesh* (the Crude Spirit that represents the lowest level of the soul), and would ascend the ladder to a higher level of *Ruach* (Spirit) which would ultimately unite with the *Ruach* of Rabbi Akiva.[30]

One Shabbat, the Ari noticed the following text on Haim Vital's forehead: "They prepared a chair for Hezkiahu, King of Judah."[31] He understood immediately that a part of the soul of Hezkiahu had joined that of Haim Vital through the mystery of *Tosfat Shabbat,* whereby one acquires on Shabbat parts of other souls which may remain for a longer or shorter time, depending on the actions of the recipient. During that Shabbat Vital became angry with a member of his family, and the additional soul consequently left him. After a week of repentance, the Ari noticed the following Shabbat the embodiment of the *Ruach*, or higher level of soul of both Hezkiahu and Rabbi Akiva in Haim Vital. Having thus attained a majestic level of spirituality, Vital was unable to prevent the influence of the left column from distracting him from his path of piety — again he quarreled with a member of his family, and again the spirits of Hezkiahu and Rabbi Akiva left him. This time, however, he repented immediately and emended the entire left column of anger, whereupon Ben Azzai, the son-in-law of Rabbi Akiva, entered his spiritual realm.[32]

The Ari considered it necessary to reveal Haim Vital's levels of spirituality to him in this way in order to explain why his exalted vessel had been chosen and prepared to receive the great light that would illumine the sublime wisdom of Kabbalah. One day Vital asked the Ari, "How can you tell me that my soul is so elevated when it is well known that even the less pious of former generations were of such a high degree of elevation that I can never hope to reach even their comparatively low level of spirituality?" The Ari replied, "The levels of spirituality are not dependent on a man's deeds or incarnated soul alone, but are in relation to the level of the generation in which he finds himself; thus a minor deed in our generation may be compared to much greater deeds in previous generations, due to the severity and dominance of the *klippot* (the shells or vessels of Evil) in the world today. Had you lived in an earlier time, therefore, these same deeds of yours would have been superior to those of the most pious of that generation. This is similar to what has been said with regard to Noah: that he was righteous in his wicked generation (Genesis 6:9); had he lived in a generation of righteous men, he would certainly have been a more righteous individual. You should not, therefore, be amazed or confused about your exalted spiritual level."[33]

On another occasion, when Vital implored the Ari to tell him why he did not devote his valuable time to more eminent scholars such as Yosef Caro, the Radvaz, the Ari's teacher, or the Alshikh, the Ari replied, "Do I really need you? Do I derive any benefit from my association with you? On the contrary, your extreme youth, compared with those scholars that you mentioned, should give me reasons to associate more closely with them, so that my reputation might be enhanced; if that were my objective, I would certainly have chosen that way. However, after considering the matter carefully, and reflecting upon these righteous persons, penetrating their innermost recesses, I find no vessel as pure and as spiritually elevated as yours. This should satisfy your curiosity; I have no intention of revealing the secrets of these men, and you should rather rejoice in your share of the spiritual realm."[34]

So it was that Haim Vital and his son Shmuel laboured together to produce the Writings of the Ari. Shmuel recorded every word transmitted to him by his father with the efficiency of an accomplished scribe, and the resulting volumes achieved great fame as the classic text-book on the Zohar.

Now just as in the case of his father Haim Vital, Shmuel Vital had also been carefully chosen to perform the tasks allocated to him in his lifetime. If we are to understand the significance of the doctrines of Kabbalah in our own times, it is important to have some understanding of the spiritual development of the Kabbalah in past ages. The characters and personalities of the Kabbalists of Safed were the channels or cables through which the power of the Kabbalah was transmitted, so that complete understanding of its wisdom is impossible unless we are aware of the spiritual composition of those who taught it, or those who set it down for future generations. This is made possible through the sublime teachings of Rabbi Shimon, later developed and elaborated upon by the Ari, regarding the transmigration of the soul.

In the *Sefer Hagilgulim* (the Book of Transmigrations), the

Ari describes the developments leading to the exile and migration of Shmuel Vital's soul and their significance in relation to the mission to which he was assigned during his life on earth. According to the Ari, there were special affinities between Haim Vital and his son. Haim's first wife was a reincarnation of Kalba Shevua, Rabbi Akiva's father-in-law; because her soul had its origins in a male, she could not bear children. As the Ari explained, "And Hannah will die, and you (Haim) will marry again when your *Nefesh* (lower aspect of the soul) is corrected, and you join the second level of the spiritual ladder, which is *Ruach.* When your *Nefesh* has enveloped that of Rabbi Akiva, your *Ruach* will become joined to his, and only then will you be permitted to marry your true soul-mate. She will be on the same spiritual plane as Rabbi Akiva's soul-mate, since your soul and that of Rabbi Akiva are truly united on the levels of *Nefesh* and *Ruach.* Then you will marry Kalba Shevua's daughter Rachel, and will be blessed with a son, whom you will call Shmuel."[35]

So far it is clear that Shmuel Vital's spiritual background was of the rarest quality; however, there is as yet no indication of why he was chosen for the specific task of recording the teachings of the Ari, as they were reported to him by his father. For this information, we must turn to Haim Vital himself:
Vital himself:

"One day Haim Vital revealed to his son that he was a reincarnation of Rabbi Meir, the celebrated *tannah.* Later Shmuel had a dream in which the Rabbi himself told him the same. It is stated in the Mishnah that Rabbi Meir was the foremost scribe of his generation. Rabbi Joseph Vital, Haim Vital's grandfather, was also blessed with a spark of the soul of Rabbi Meir, and he too was a noted scribe. Haim Vital says of his grandfather that he was one of the greatest scribes the world has ever known. 'The Ari told me,' he said to his son, 'that at one time half the world received spiritual nourishment through the merits of our grandfather, because of the accuracy and faithfulness with which, in his position as scribe, he prepared the written portion of Tefillin.

You, my son, are incarnated with that spark as well, which is why you are able to record the words of the Ari with such accuracy.[36]

Shmuel Vital was ideally suited to his task, as indeed, were his father Haim Vital and their teacher, the Ari. Through the spiritual vessel of Shmuel the world was now prepared to enter the Messianic era, fully equipped with all the necessary material and knowledge to carry out the work required of it; however, despite the fact that a complete commentary on the Zohar was now available, the metaphors and interwoven imagery were still understood only by a select few.

While it is true to say that the Lurianic system provides the necessary background for a full and comprehensive understanding of the Zohar, it is nonetheless puzzling that Haim Vital should have almost totally ignored the commentaries of the master Kabbalist, Moses Cordovero, the Ari's mentor. According to legend the reason lies in a dream that Haim Vital once had in which Moses Cordovero appeared before him and told him that, although both his system and that of the Ari were correct interpretations of the Zohar, the Ari's would prevail in Messianic era. This in fact, is the case today, when the Writings of the Ari have been arranged, organised and published, while those of the Ramak (Rabbi Moses Cordovero) have only recently been rediscovered.

Another famous Kabbalist who flourished during the Golden Age of enlightenment which lasted from about 1490 until 1590 was Abraham ben Mordechai Azulai (1570-1643). Born in Fez to a family of Kabbalists of Castilian origin, he wrote three treatises based on the Zohar: *Or haLevanah* (Light of the Moon), Or haHamah (Light of the Sun), and *Or haganuz* (the Hidden Light), all three being based primarily on the Lurianic system; he also prepared a volume entitled *Hesed l'Avraham* (the Mercy of Abraham), in which he presented an analysis of the principles of Kabbalah.

The words of his preface to *Or haHamah* ring with greater force today than ever before. "It is most important from this time on that everyone study the Kabbalah publicly and preoccupy themselves with it. For, by the merit of Kabbalah — in fact, solely through Kabbalah — will the Messiah appear and efface forever war, destruction, social injustice and, above all, man's inhumanity to his fellow man."

It may be said, therefore, that the Spanish Inquisition, for all its violence, ushered in the Golden Age of Enlightenment, and that the Lurianic era set the stage for the Messianic age.

CHAPTER V

A LATER LIGHT — RABBI ASHLAG

Despite the growth and influence of Hassidism with its renewed interest in Kabbalah, it would still be true to say that the majority of Jews remained as ignorant of the teachings of Kabbalah as ever. This situation began to change, however, when Rabbi Yehuda Ashlag (1886-1955) pioneered a new system for understanding the works of the Ari. In his sixteen-volume textbook, the *Study of the Ten Luminous Emanations (Talmud Eser hasfirot)* he devised a logical system through which the essence of the transcendent realm was transmitted by means of an array of symbols and illustrations. These, he felt, best described those aspects of the teachings of the Ari that were beyond the grasp of the intellect alone. The *Ten Luminous Emanations* deals with those concepts that have eluded the most determined scholars for centuries. The intimate relationship between the physical and metaphysical realms is presented simply, together with a description of the series of evolutions that culminates in the world we know today, and also a detailed presentation of those motives that may be ascribed to the Creator.

In addition to these volumes, Rabbi Ashlag's monumental work on the Zohar has had a great influence on Judaic studies and marks a turning-point in the attempt to render the Kabbalah comprehensible to contemporary students. His was the first translation of the entire Zohar into modern Hebrew. Realising that a comprehensive translation would not be sufficient on its own, he also composed a commentary on the most difficult passages. He compiled too a volume of diagrams describing the process of evolution of the *Sefirot* in all their manifestations down to the level of this world.

Generally speaking, Kabbalists of the rank and stature of Rabbi Ashlag receive their knowledge through Divine revelation. They tend to be men with a broad rabbinic education, and Rabbi Ashlag was no exception in this respect. More penetrating, however, was his knowledge of the spectrum of Kabbalah, and his translation of the Zohar shows clearly that he was knowledgeable in every known science.

I was told of his life and personality by my master Rabbi Yehuda Z. Brandwein, who was his disciple. Rabbi Ashlag was born in Warsaw and educated in Hassidic schools. In his early years, he was a student of Shalom Rabinowicz of Kalushin and of his son Yehoshah Asher of Porissor. He emigrated to Palestine in 1919 and settled in the Old City of Jerusalem. Rabbi Brandwein told of a man with immense powers of meditation, a man to whom the worlds of metaphysics and mysticism were as familiar as was the world of physics to Einstein. The comparison is not altogether without significance, since it was during Rabbi Ashlag's lifetime that great advances and discoveries were being made in the world of science, destroying many of the traditional scientific theories of stability, permanence and purpose in the universe. The great monument of that scientific era, Einstein's Theory of Relativity, confirmed what Kabbalists had known to be true for centuries — that time, space and motion are not immutable constants but a function of energy.

The increasing awareness among scientists of the shortcomings of the analytic methodology of science and the growing sense of the unity and inter-relatedness of physical and biological systems has given a fresh impetus to the world of mysticism, and particularly to Kabbalah. In this respect, the works of Rabbi Ashlag are distinguished by their unique and striking mixture of salient facts concerning the structure of the universe, together with a deep, penetrating description of the purpose of the individual within this system.

The restoration of a mystical approach in the world of Kabbalah, as opposed to the dry study of ritual and ceremony for their own sake, draws a large part of its strength from the link between the concepts expressed and the mystical consciousness of the author. Since the beginnings of Kabbalah the Prophet Elijah has been closely identified with its profound teachings. He appeared to both Rabbi Shimon and the Ari. Rabbi Ashlag, however, did not claim Elijah as the source of his mystical revelation. A beautiful story, told to me by my master, demonstrates the inner connection that existed between the soul of Rabbi Ashlag and the levels on high: "One evening," recalled the Rabbi, "following the completion of a volume of the Zohar, I dozed off into a very deep slumber. A voice came to me and proclaimed that I would be shown the entire Creation, from the beginning to the very end, including the coming of the Messiah. I then asked why I could not be shown that which the prophets had seen. The reply was, Why should you be satisfied with the visionary level of the prophets, when you can see all?"

The source of his revelation is described in a letter written by Rabbi Ashlag to an uncle,[37] in which he relates his meeting with his master, and the aura egocentricity that he developed after learning the inner mysteries of the Kabbalah. This element of pride led to his master discontinuing the lessons until Rabbi Ashlag had adopted the correct attitude of humility, whereupon his master — a stranger whose name he was forbidden to utter — revealed to him a *Sod* (a secret or inner meaning) concerning the *Mikveh* (ritual bath). "This," reports Rabbi Ashlag, "brought on an ecstasy of such intensity that it literally created a total *Devekut,* a cleaving to the Divine Essence, a complete separation from corporeality, and a tearing asunder of the veil of eternal life." Shortly after this revelation his master passed away, leaving him brokenhearted. As a result of his deep sorrow and despair the revelation, too, left him for a while, until he was once more able to devote his life to the Creator, "Whereupon the fountains of heavenly wisdom suddenly burst forth, (and)

with the grace of the Almighty, I remembered all the revelations
I had received from my master, of blessed memory."

Today, as in the Golden Age of Safed, the invisible spring of
Kabbalah has once again come to the surface; in our times,
however, we notice one significant difference — science, for so
long the sworn enemy of all religion, can now be seen in its true
light as the ally and companion of Kabbalah.

CHAPTER VI

KABBALAH AND THE AGE OF THE MESSIAH

Before delving more deeply into the actual methodology and teaching of Kabbalah, let us look in greater detail at the suggestions already made as to the appropriateness of its study at this time; in particular, it is necessary to understand the connection between the study of Kabbalah and the approach of the Messianic Age.

We have already had cause to observe the rising tide of interest in occult teachings and in the Zohar, together with the reawakening of spirituality within Judaism and other religions. The inevitable question is then raised as to why the Zohar was effectively concealed from earlier generations, since they were undoubtedly at a more conscious and spiritual level than our own and thus better equipped to understand the Kabbalah's profound wisdom.

A clue to the solution of this problem is provided by the Zohar, in a discourse on the coming of the Messiah: "Rabbi Shimon raised his hands and wept and said, "Woe unto him who meets with that period; praiseworthy is the portion of him who encounters and has the divine capacity to be cast with that time." Rabbi Shimon then explains this paradoxical remark as follows: "Who unto him who meets with that period, for when the Almighty shall remember the *Shechina* (the Divine Presence), if He shall gaze upon those who stand loyal to her, upon all who are found in her midst, and then scrutinize the actions and deeds of each, He will not find among them a single right - ous one, as the scripture warns, 'I looked, and there was none to help.' Agonizing torment and trouble lie in wait for Israel.

Praiseworthy, however, are those who shall merit the joy-giving light of the King. Concerning that time, it is proclaimed. 'I will refine them as silver is refined, I shall try them as gold is tried.'[38]

Rabbi Shimon confirmed that the Messianic Era will bring with it a Light and a richness representing the infusion of Divine purity through all the worlds. The dawn of a new world will appear, and with its advent, the Light will begin to liberate men from their ignorance, bringing them a spiritual and intellectual awakening. The rich residue of moral and spiritual inspiration latent in our Jewish heritage will arouse the need for reconstruction and reorganisation, and will direct our energies into channels that will ultimately contribute toward the enrichment of Jewish experience and our relationship with our fellow men.[39]

The Zohar also states that, in the days of the Messiah, "There will no longer be the necessity for one to request of his neighbour, 'Teach me wisdom,' as it is written, 'One day they will no longer teach every man his neighbour, and every man his brother, saying Know the Lord, for they shall all know Me, from the youngest to the oldest of them.'"[40]

The Zohar here expresses the idea that the Messianic era will usher in a period of unprecedented enlightenment: Messianism, representing the essence of hope and optimism, grows out of the indelible belief that there will be an eventual triumph of world harmony over confusion, of love over hate, an ultimate victory of justice and kindness over oppression and greed. This victory, declares the Zohar, is inextricably bound to *Hochma* (wisdom), and dependent upon the dissemination of true knowledge, the sublime wisdom of the Kabbalah.

However, taken all together, these facts still do not reveal the ultimate cause of the Messianic disturbances and perplexities involving the Light of the Messiah and final redemption. Neither have they explained or answered the closely related question of why the Kabbalah was not revealed in its full glory to earlier generations. Why now? Is our confused generation in some way better suited to receive the abundance of Light, to savour the ineffable Beneficence awaiting the souls present in our age, the Messianic period?

Such paradoxes regarding the relative merit of earlier and latter generations were dealt with in the Talmud by our sages of blessed memory: "Rav Pappa said to Abbaye, 'How is it that miracles were performed for earlier generations, yet no wonders are produced for us?' It cannot be due to their superiority in study, since in the years of Rav Yehuda (a sage of an earlier generation) the aggregate of their studies was confined to the order of *Nezikins* (the fourth of six books of the Mishnah) whereas we study all six orders: in fact, when Rav Yehuda came to the tractate of *Uktzin,* he would say, I see here all the difficulties raised by Rav and Shmuel; we on the other hand, possess thirteen versions of this same tractate. Then again, when Rav Yehuda drew off one of his shoes (before fasting for rain), rain used to start falling immediately, whereas we torment ourselves and cry out, yet no recognition is accorded us.' To this Abbaye replied, 'The former generations were prepared to sacrifice their lives for the sanctification of the name of the Lord.'"[41]

It was obvious to Rav Pappa and Abbaye that earlier generations were infinitely superior to them from the standpoint of the immortal inner soul; however, from the point of view of the revelations of Torah, knowledge and wisdom, Rav Pappa and Abbaye were the greater beneficiaries of this vast reservoir of Divine literature than were earlier generations.

The discussion in the Talmud anticipates the questions being raised in this generation. It is concerned with the nature of spirituality and its change over the span of time. In their discussions the sages show that they are fully aware of the paradox at the centre of the issue; the earlier generations, being more spiritual by nature, needed less in the way of spiritual knowledge from books, yet achieved more in the realm of the working of wonders and miracles. Thus we find a situation where greater knowledge and more intensive study appears to be less rewarded. The resolution of this paradox lies in the spiritual level achieved in different generations. The earlier generations are, quite simply, closer to the source of spirituality than the later ones; they demand far less from the physical world — both physically and spiritually, they are on a higher plane of existence. Being thus less dependent on the mundane vessels of the physical world, they could maintain their elevated status, and indeed exert control over the direction of the world, through their spirituality. The expression of this control was the manifestation of 'miracles', meaning the display of their power over the natural order of the universe. Later generations have to rely to a greater extent on knowledge from secondary sources, such as the written word; at the same time, their greater dependence on the world — their Desire to Receive — makes them more capable of receiving the Light, which is of the highest nature. The vessels to receive that Light are of a coarser material, but the Light, once it has penetrated, is present in a much more explicit form than in former generations. Instead of one book — six books. Instead of just Mishnah, — Talmud. Instead of just Talmud — Zohar.

R. Shimon then said: 'There are three signs in a man: paleness is a sign of anger, talking is a sign of folly, and selfpraise is a sign of ignorance'.

Zohar III, P. 193b.

PART TWO

THE BODY OF KNOWLEDGE

'*If a man* loves *a woman who lives in a street of*
tanners, *if she were not there he would never go into
it, but because she is there it seems to him like a
street of spice makers where all the* sweet scents *of
the world are to be found. So "even when they are in
the land of their enemies", which is the street of
tanners, "I will not abhor or reject them", because of
that bride in their midst, the beloved of my soul who
abides there*'.

Zohar III, P. 115b.

CHAPTER VII

THE METHODOLOGY OF KABBALAH

Contemporary models of methodology stem for the most part from one or another of the many branches of science and technology, where increasingly sophisticated and complex techniques are being invented for the gathering and analysis of information; yet the further scientific endeavour progresses down its chosen path, the more its methods seem to hinder its objectives. Today we have reached a stage where the language and terminology of the scientist is incomprehensible to the layman, and often to scientists in other fields as well. The scientist-philosopher of earlier generations who understood how his area of study fitted in with the structure of the universe has given way to the specialist, who limits his field of view in the vain hope of being able to master some small corner of the physical world. The hope is vain, according to the teachings of the Kabbalah, because the physical world to which science has restricted itself is a world of effects. The true causes lay beyond it in the realm of the metaphysical. Even so, there are a number of assumptions made by the scientific method that give the lie to its claims of objectivity, by far the greatest being the assumption that the universe is ordered, and that it obeys the law of cause and effect. Neither of these fundamentals, without which science cannot exist, can be substantiated without recourse to knowledge of higher non-physical modes of existence.

Even within these self-imposed restrictions, there are limits to the scope of the scientific method, on its own, it is incapable of generating new ideas. Max Planck, the renowned physicist wrote in his autobiography: "When the pioneer in science sends forth the groping fingers of his thoughts, he must have a vivid, intuitive imagination, for new ideas are not generated by deduction, but by an artistically creative imagination."[42]

Without the subjective element of imagination then, the objectives of science cannot be reached. But how 'scientific' can science be if it depends on an impetus that, by its very definition, is unscientific?

The question is, perhaps, unfair; we are too ready to categorise ideas and principles, forgetting often that our categories are arbitrarily selected. Thus we think of science as dealing with knowledge, as its etymological root might suggest, and religion or philosophy as being concerned with truth or essence; the reality is not so cut-and-dried, and we find that all these disciplines attempt to arrive at a balanced combination of knowledge and truth together. This combination is the wisdom referred to by the sages, as we have seen, as 'seeing the consequences of action.'

At the basis of this quest for wisdom lies the question of method: 'how shall I know?' It is at this point that many feel that science and religion part company; thus, it is the claim of many modern thinkers that the advances in science are a direct result of the decline of religion as a force in the world. A kabbalistic interpretation of history would challenge this assumption on the grounds that the implied distinction between knowledge and faith, together with the implied superiority of the former over the latter, is altogether false.

Contemporary scientific thought and writing on the subject of the scientific method show clearly that it is not the all-powerful tool that was once hoped. Perception, psychologists have finally realised, is an active process of sorting and interpreting, and not the passive, 'objective' absorption of stimuli implied by the scientific method. We must, in other words have a priori knowledge — a concept that comes very close to the idea of faith — before we can see and understand. In the Kabbalah, there is no rigid distinction between physical and spiritual forms, and the picture presented is one of a total, unified, interrelated system. The priori knowledge that casts doubt on the objectivity of science appears here in the form of the Desire to Receive, whereby we have a tendency to project onto 'reality' what we want to see, rather than what might actually exist. This distinction between the projections of our physical bodies (the outward appearance) and the essence lies at the root of the difference of approach between science and Kabbalah. Science asks only how something exists within the dimensions or limitations of time, space, motion and causality; Kabbalah goes further and confronts the question of why things exist at all.

Having made this point, it should be said that modern science is increasingly coming to the realisation that there are interesting and profitable areas of study that are not governed by the laws of time, space and motion. Instead of observation of interactions, supported by formulae and equations, the emphasis is shifting to the study of subtle and indefinable changes, so small that they may not follow the accepted behavior of the physical world. Perhaps, after all, physical reality no longer represents the final word in scientific disclosure.

The interpretation of the universe to be found in the Zohar stresses not only the polarities of existence — time and timelessness, motion and motionlessness — but also the role played by man himself as a causative factor. Here we find a description of the true scientist, the vital link played by man in the chain of discovery that stretches from the potential of knowledge in the universe down to its manifestation on earth. In this view, the scientist is as much a part of the universe as his discovery; indeed, he is a part of what he discovers, since he acts as a channel for the knowledge of his discovery. Thus we can no longer ignore the psyche of the scientist, the searcher after wisdom, and must take this additional variable into consideration when approaching theoretical physical phenomena. This brings in further problems, drawing us nearer to the mysterious unknown. The question remains, however: is it possible to reach the ultimate goal of absolute truth, and if it is, how does one set about it?

We see an apple seed being planted. We assume that, the laws of cause and effect being usually reliable, the apple tree and eventually the fruit will appear in due course. This is similar to the course of events in the realm of metaphysics, where, undetected by any physical means, the delicate interplay of cause and effect is at work. Through the precepts, laws, commandments, prohibitions, allegories and tales of the Torah and Talmud, Kabbalah teaches us about the workings of the unseen world. The outcome of man's actions, the consequences of his motivations, are expressed in metaphors of reward and punishment. The Kabbalah reveals the mystical interpretation of the Torah's use of retribution, atonement and suffering. The function of this knowledge is radically different from that of science: it allows us to recognize the paths by which all creative processes emanate from G-d, Who is the root of all Creation — albeit the hidden root. In the phsyical world, the interaction of unknown elements may at times be revealed to the scientists; the essence of those elements which creates the interactions is nevertheless completely obscured from the perception of the five senses. The strings of formulae and equations may describe the interactions — the effects — but these tools can never reveal the innermost secrets of the reasons for the reaction.

It is the task of Kabbalah, especially in its current state of development, to provide such bridges and connections between the physical world of How? and the spiritual world of Why?

The language of Kabbalah is the language of man; it permits us to appreciate its profound wisdom to the utmost extent of our capabilities. To a generation that has witnessed numberless advances in every sphere of scientific research, the wisdom of Kabbalah can no longer be considered remote and inaccessible; on the contrary, its most important teachings are becoming increasingly vital to a growing number of people who find themselves adrift in a strange and confusing technological world.

We come now to another area of difference between science and Kabbalah, an area which in itself suggests why many people believe Kabbalah to be even more complicated and inaccessible than science. The difference may be understood by considering the relationships that exist between objects. When we wish to make a distinction between two objects or events, because we can see no connection between them, we say that they are unrelated, that their occurrence or presence together is coincidental. The root meaning of this word "coincidental', however, has quite the opposite meaning — it implies that our two objects, have, occurred together. The teachings of Kabbalah indicate that the second sense, apart from being literal, is also the true one — since two events that occur together, in whatever dimension (time, space, thought, etc.), are related to one another. The question now arises of how this difference in interpretation arose. The answer is that science, however deeply it penetrates into the world of the senses, is still only dealing with external phenomena. The scientist's world is the manifest universe — a universe, in which the outward structures remain purely secondary in importance. It is the task of the scientist to examine and report the outer surface, whereas the Kabbalist is concerned with pointing out the alignments ('coincidences') of one world with the other, locating and strengthening the links between the world of appearances and the world of essence.

If, as we have said, the fundamental concern of the Kabbalah is with the Desire to Receive, it follows from the foregoing that its task must be to reveal the nature of this force, and the ways in which it is connected with the material world. Not to do so would imply a separation between the two worlds that does not exist. Here, however, there is an obvious dilemma, since the inner or supernal world is described in the Zohar as being without form or outer covering — that which we refer to colloquially as 'the naked truth' — and cannot therefore be described directly by means of the outer coverings with which we are familiar in this material world. This is the Sod (secret) of truth, the Essence of all elements, which is never affected by change or movement but remains the prime causative factor in all interactions. We can more easily understand this concept if we imagine curtains or veils of various colours placed between us and the sun; what we see is a change in the appearance of the light as it is filtered through the different coloured curtains, but, clearly, the actual light of the sun does not alter. The essence of any thing, being without form, remains beyond the grasp of rational thought, and as such cannot be communicated through ordinary languages or familiar levels of experience; only after it has become interwoven with the external world of material existence can it be perceived, although even then it remains elusive and deceptive.

Mysticism relates to that which is without form. The sublime wisdom of the Kabbalah has thus become known as Jewish mysticism, since it attempts to provide us with an understanding of essence and truth through which a clearer perspective of our actions may be reached. Once we have achieved an understanding of the root or essence of any element, the subsequent interactions resulting from these basic elements will, of necessity, behave within the limits of the root, according to the principle that the branch (effect or interaction) and the root (cause) will always be in harmony. With this knowledge of essence we can avoid many of the conflicting and opposing viewpoints that hinder our progress and understanding, both as individuals and as nations.

Within the esoteric teachings of the Kabbalah, we set foot on that road of the essence, the root, the point of view which alone can show us the straight and narrow path that leads to the Absolute. Once we can recognise the realm of the real, where the veils of the material world are stripped away, we may achieve universal oneness; having unveiled the mysteries and enigmas of life, we shall reach total truth. Hence the names *Wisdom of the Mysterious* and *Wisdom of the Truth* have been given to the Zohar to denote the motif of this great work, the treasury of the Jewish mystical world of ideas.

This, then, is the distinction between science and Kabbalah. Even though both claim to be searching for truth, their expectations and criteria — and therefore their findings — are different. Kabbalah posits the existence of two basic levels of life — spiritual and material — and treats them both as proper subjects of investigation and analysis. It suggests too that, rather than being separate, there are strong and necessary links between the two, and that the Desire to Receive acts as a common link. The results of the Desire to Receive can, of course, be seen in the external world of appearances to which science has chosen to limit itself. However, the Desire itself cannot be observed scientifically, since the world of the scientist — whether dealing with astronomy or sub-atomic physics — is one of outward effects, the prime causes always remaining hidden. To rely on the findings of science alone is tacitly to accept the view that the external world is self-contained and self-constructed, yet the further we delve into the mysteries of the physical universe, the more we become aware that such an interpretation just does not fit the information we now have at our disposal. The Kabbalah presents an alternative view to this mechanistic philosophy of existence, one that sees man as the ultimate missing link between the upper and lower worlds. That link, technically speaking, is in our very blood, which contains not only material substances but also the lowest spiritual level of the Desire to Receive — as it is written:[43] *'hadam hu hanefesh'*, the blood is the soul.

With its central core of symbolism, the Zohar reveals the essence of *Nistar* (the mysterious) as timeless, changeless, motionless and eternal. Material phenomena, distinguished by the characteristic of Being in the realm of reality, are perceived by our physical channels of perception, while those things that are beyond the range of our senses can be observed in part through interaction. This explains why, since each individual can either consciously or unconsciously interpret his individual experiences through his own selective reasoning, the interactions of material phenomena may be differently understood.

Conditions for Studying Kabbalah

The claims made in this work for the study of Kabbalah are admittedly large; indeed, it is hard to imagine larger. This is because Kabbalah deals with ultimate reality, the ultimate truth of man's essence, so that no claim can be too great. On the other hand, the very power generated by this knowledge might suggest that it would be wiser to restrict its availability to those who would best be able to handle it. It is therefore necessary to remind ourselves of the divisions and scope of Kabbalah.

Kabbalists such as Rabbi Shimon Bar Yohai, Moses Cordovero and Isaac Luria, and many others in days past who possessed the secrets of *Sitrei Torah* were capable of transcending the physical realm altogether. It was through the power of *Sitrei Torah* that many of the legendary incidents in their lives were affected. The traditional prohibitions on the study of *Sitrei Torah* should not, however, be seen as placing chains and impediments on man's freedom of thought; on the contrary, there is no place in Torah for the suppression of inquiry and knowledge. Is it conceivable that a Jew should be required to observe precepts and commandments, yet be prohibited from understanding them to the utmost extent of his ability? Why, then, were such stringent conditions imposed before one could enter the portals of *Sitrei Torah?*

We must realise that, unless the intellect has been properly trained and prepared, there are areas in which the mind does not and cannot have a total grasp. This could be compared to attempting to explain the concept of light to a man who has been blind from birth — the explanation will have no meaning for him, since the concept is one of which he has no knowledge. The inner depths of man, the subconscious mind, remain irrevocably sealed to the probing of the intellect; to avoid confusion and frustration, which might eventually lead to negating the precepts and commandments of the Torah, our sages' prohibition was in effect a warning to the student that he was incapable of attaining this knowledge, so that the pursuit of *Sitrei Torah* would be pointless.

It would be foolish to rely on human intellect and reason alone as a passport to the Divine mysteries of *Sitrei Torah;* the preconditions laid down by the sages are necessary before one can find the entrance to the sanctuary — without them one would wander about lost and groping in the darkness. It is clearly stated that one must be over forty years old to study these secrets, as well as being male and married. The initiate into this realm must also be well versed in all aspects of Torah study (Talmud and Mishna), and must have a thirst for the knowledge of the secrets that makes his life unbearable without it. This knowledge, without Divine guidance, remains hidden. Thus we find some sections of the Zohar marked as containing *Sitrei Torah:* this means that unless the conditions have been met and the gates of this knowledge have been opened, the true meaning of these passages will not be perceived.

However, to study the reasons for the precepts and rituals of the Torah, known as *Ta'amei Torah,* was not only possible but was even encouraged by the sages. To understand the order and purpose of Creation leads to the very root of one's existence and being. The individual striving to grasp the moral essence of unity with the Divine Spirit was provided with the proper and necessary tools — namely the commandments of Torah — to achieve this unification with the Divine Light. A precise and methodical system, originating within the framework of the Zohar, meticulously researched and compiled by the Ari and accompanied by Divine Revelation from Elijah the Prophet, furnished new dimensions of understanding regarding the *Mitzvot* of the Torah and concepts of spirituality. The Lurianic system emerged as a way of joining together human emotion, thus providing spiritual nourishment for all those whose natures contained aspects of these two forces. The scientist, in his pursuit of reason and his unfailing faith in logic, will find in *Ta'amei Torah* the unity of mind and heart that lie at the very centre of the sublime mysteries of the Torah. The genuinely religious person, needing no confirmation that all the teaching of the Torah are both Divinely inspired and true, will now find and understand the inner meaning and purposes of the precepts revealed by G-d on Mount Sinai. Each prayer and *Mitzvah* will then reveal forces that unite the physical and metaphysical worlds. The pious observant man, constantly struggling with apparent inconsistencies and contradictions when confronting the problem of good and evil, will in *Ta'amei Torah* find solutions so profound that they will completely satisfy all his doubts. This should not be taken to imply that complete reliance on one's own thought processes will necessarily reveal the totality of this sublime wisdom; however, one need not be apprehensive when considering the variety of questions that may plague the inquisitive rationalist, since it would be unthinkable for the Torah to forbid the acquisition of knowledge through inquiry, containing as it does the answers to all possible questions.

Wisdom is an integral branch of the Torah, despite the limitations that permeate the fibre of man's finite being; closing the doors of Kabbalah because of the few who have followed false paths would be like forbidding the *Kiddush* over wine because of those individuals who have unfortunately become addicted to alcohol. If the profound study of *Ta'ami Torah* permits and encourages inquiries into and comprehension of the precepts and commandments, then it is incumbent upon each of us to pursue and acquire this knowledge with the utmost zeal. Ignorance of the paths of Torah and of its inner meaning will eventually lead to contempt and neglect: without wisdom and understanding, religion — and ultimately, life itself — is meaningless. In the same way, abstract knowledge and intellectual attainment alone, divorced from a practical moral philosophy and the fulfillment of *Mitzvot* contained in the Torah, cannot provide spiritual nourishment for the thirsting soul.

The Biblical Methods of Kabbalah

Though Kabbalah often deals with profound matters, it does so in language that can be easily understood, a process which in itself contains an important lesson. The method of dissemination of knowledge in the Kabbalah points to one of its central teachings, namely that the Divine word of infinity can be transformed into the finite and limited language of man.

This method is not exclusive to the Kabbalah. Its roots are to be found in earlier written texts, particularly in those of Mishnah, and even earlier in the writing of the Torah itself. Both of these contain not only directives and imperatives but also, perhaps less expectedly, stories, songs, parables and histories, which would seem at first to have no logical place in such work.

For the Kabbalists, the stories of the Torah are merely the outer covering under which exalted mysteries are concealed. They are only the garment for the body of the inner meaning. The Kabbalah seeks to imbue the commandments and laws of the Torah with their true, hidden spirit. Indeed, in the view of the Zohar the tales and parables of the Torah are symbolic reflections of the inner metaphysical realm through which one could perceive the hidden, divine mysteries of our universe. Rabbi Shimon berates those who take these simple tales as relating only to incidents in the lives of individuals or nations.

"Rabbi Shimon said, 'Woe unto the man who says that Torah merely presents narratives and mundane matters. For, if it is the nature of the Torah that it only deals with simple matters, we, in our day, could compile a superior version; if the Torah comes just to inform us of everyday things, then there are in the possession of the rulers of the world books of greater quality, and from these we could copy and compose a Torah. However, the uniqueness of the Torah lies in the fact that each word contains supernal matters and profound secrets.

'See how precisely balanced are the upper and lower worlds; Israel here below is the equivalent of the angels above, about whom it is written, Who maketh his angels into winds (Psalms 104:4). When the angels descend, they enclothe themselves in earthly garments, without which they could not exist in this world, nor could it bear to co-exist with them if they were not thus clothed. If this is so with angels, then how much more must it be true of the Torah* and all the worlds, the Torah through which all are sustained? The world could not endure the Torah had she not enclothed herself in the garments of this world (tales and narratives)'.

'Tales related in the Torah are merely the Torah's outer garments: one who considers the outer garments as the Torah itself and no more is a simpleton, and will not merit a portion in the world to come. King David said, Open my eyes, that I may behold wondrous things from your Torah (Psalms 119:18), the meaning of which is that one should perceive that which lies beneath the outer garment of the Torah.

'The clothes man wears are the most visible part of him: fools, on seeing a well-dressed man, do not see any further, and judge him simply on the basis of his beautiful clothes. They see the attire as a reflection of the physical individual, and the physical appearance as a reflection of the soul itself.

'So it is with the Torah: its narrations relating to the mundane things of this world are but the garments which clothe the body of the Torah; the body of the Torah consists of its *Mitzvot* (precepts). Foolish people see the outer garment, the narrations of the Torah, and ignore that which lies beneath this outer garment. Those who understand more see the body beneath the garment, but the truly wise, however, those who serve the supernal King and who stood on Mount Sinai, will penetrate to the soul (of the Torah) which is the essence of the entire Torah itself'."[44]

When Rabbi Shimon says, "When the angels descend, they enclothe themselves in earthly garments....." (above), he reveals

---

* In as much as the angels were created *from* the Torah.

two significant *Sodot* (secrets) in relation to the conceptual reality of mysticism. Spirituality, indicated in the Zohar by the term 'angels', cannot reveal anything of its essence unless it is clothed by a corporeal garment. It is only when it is thus enclothed that the outward actions and interactions reveal something of their essence through the five senses. It is largely through these five senses that we develop the formulae and exploratory devices that enable us to evaluate and store data relating to the external world.

The thoughts of man, before being put into the corporeal garment of speech, remain hidden within the mind of the individual. As a thought is revealed through this corporeal garment of speech, a stranger phenomenon takes place, both in relation to the speaker and the listener. The original thought or idea in the mind may emerge in quite a different form, with quite a different sense, when it is passed through the 'filter' of speech. Neither will the words reaching the ears of the listener necessarily correspond to those uttered by the speaker. Indeed, it is remarkable how many divergent points of view can arise among a number of listeners from an idea expressed by one individual. Taken one step further, we might pass a voice through the medium of a telephone or tape-recorder, whereupon the resulting distortion will often appear to the original speaker to be the voice of someone else; thus we see how misleading the forms of the mundane world can be.

However, cautions Rabbi Shimon, without these earthly garments — the cables and vessels — metaphysical essence could not co-exist with, or be observed by this world; this is why the Zohar concerns itself with the study of essence, providing instant understanding of its characteristics, and thereby avoiding the potential inaccuracies and misinterpretations that inevitably arise from the study of the earthly garments of action and interaction.

This then is the first Sod revealed by Rabbi Shimon: that metaphysical concepts and essence are, and must be, enclothed in corporeal garments, and that all actions and interactions that we observe consist of, and are governed by metaphysical forces.

Now to the second Sod contained in this passage of the Zohar, which is contained in the section, 'nor could it bear to co-exist with them if they were not thus clothed'. To explain this subtle but penetrating secret, let us consider the case of electricity. We know that electric current is an energy force that must be contained within some sort of cable for it to be useful. In the case of a fallen power-line or a broken cable, there is the danger of electric shock or fire, since the flowing current is no longer contained, and anything with which it comes into contact will be unable to contain this naked energy. Within the metaphysical realm, the pattern is identical: there is a great danger here when an imbalance exists between imparting positive forces and receiving negative forces. The overloading of an electrical cable (the overstraining of an individual's mental capacities) signals trouble, since the receptacle or vessel simply lacks the proper insulation and safeguards for the directed output of energy (the flow of ideas). These analogies are relevant at the peripheral areas of angelic, or pure essence of spirituality: how much greater, then, is the need for a suitable medium or garment in transmitting the omnipotent beneficence and sublime esoteric wisdom of metaphysics!

The Zohar, interwoven with profound philosophic views, reveals that the biblical narratives are the vehicles by which the Divine mysteries of our universe can be undestood. Furthermore, through a system of laws and commandments, which act as a garment for true spirituality, the same objective is achieved — as is seen in the beauty of spiritual meditation clothed in a garment of systemised prayer, or in the holiness of the Sabbath, when its metaphysical implications are fully understood.

The question of how we can be certain of the interpretation of the metaphysical plane that is revealed by the Zohar is carefully considered by its author: "And for those persons that do not know, yet have a desire to understand," declares the Zohar, "reflect upon that which is revealed and made manifest (in this world), and you shall know that which is concealed, inasmuch as everything (both above and below) is the same. For all that G-d has created in a corporeal way has been patterned after that which is above."[45]

Thus we learn the sublime teaching that when the Kabbalah reveals the essence of unseen elements, its interpretation of the concealed will not and cannot conflict with subsequent revealing actions and interactions. We are presented by the Zohar, therefore, with instant, immediate knowledge of the root of any matter, obviating the necessity of going through the customary procedures of trial and error, action and reaction, and independently of the fluctuations of time, space and motion.

CHAPTER VIII

THE MAIN TEACHINGS

The vast scope and quantity of Kabbalistic literature should not prevent us from examining some of the main ideas and concepts in a concise form, bearing in mind at all times that such a shortening does have its limitations, and is chiefly intended for the newcomer to Kabbalah. In this task, we are served well by Rabbi Ashlag, whose comprehensive works impose some order on the often complex and diffuse thoughts of the Zohar. It should be noted that the wisdom of the Kabbalah is anything but dogmatic; at all times it is left to the reader to make his choice of whether to believe, or not, using the standards set down in the previous section. Very little is left to supposition or suggestive thinking, the central aim being always clear understanding and comprehension.

There is one premise in the whole of Kabbalah, and only one. This premise, from which every idea contained in Kabbalistic teaching can be evolved, is that G-d is all-inclusive, and that He lacks nothing whatsoever. The immediate conclusion that we can draw from this statement is that He is good, since as we shall shortly demonstrate, all aspects of evil stem from the root of unfulfillment. We can see this in our own lives, where all our jealousies, anger and hatred are a result of desires for emotional or physical gratification that is not forthcoming.

Having said that G-d is complete and therefore good, we can now go on to describe the attribute through which we are aware of His existence — His desire to share. This is an extension of His goodness and is described in the Kabbalah as the Light. Again we know that sharing, or imparting, is an attribute of goodness from our experience in this mundane world. If we consider any object or person that we would call 'good', we will realise that the essential quality that all 'good' things have in common is that they give us something that we want. That 'something' might be physical, as in the case of a benefactor who gives us physical gifts, or it might be an experience that gives us pleasure. The aspect of fulfilling a part of our desires remains the constant common factor. We call this factor 'positive energy', since the positive force is always the one that is complete and tends to fill areas of incompleteness, or negativity. This positive energy is also called the Desire to Impart, or the Desire to Share. The word Desire is used because it reminds us that there can be no sharing of something we do not possess; thus we could paraphrase the Desire to Impart in the form of a Want to Give, expressing the sublime principle that the whole of existence is sustained from moment to moment only by the continuous gift of life from the Creator, fulfilling our 'want' or Desire so that we can 'give' or Impart.

This is the total of all that we can know or say about G-d: that He is complete and lacks nothing, that He is good, that His attribute is the Desire to Impart, and that the manifestation of that desire is called positive energy.

It might be thought that sharing, which is the only aspect through which the Creator is made known to us, implies diminishing; our experience in this world is that, after we have shared or given something we are left with less then before. In fact, this is often not the case, since sharing is the prerequisite for receiving. When we share, we create the correct metaphysical atmosphere for the drawing down of forces and energies from above. Nonetheless, we can safely say that a bottle of water from which half the contents are poured into another receptacle will contain less after the transaction than before. Can we then say that the Creator is diminished, G-d forbid, by his sharing with us? We have already suggested the answer in the example given above. The bottle is inanimate, and, although it contains some small degree of the Desire to Receive — without which it could not exist — it does not have the power to draw down metaphysical energy for itself; when it shares, therefore, it is diminished. When we share, as we have said, we may appear to have lost something, but we differ from the inanimate order of existence in that our Desire to Receive is far greater and is even increased each time we share; thus our apparent loss in the physical world is balanced by a gain in metaphysical power. A second example we might consider is that of a candle, whose light can light infinite number of other candles without being diminished. To be sure the candle itself will grow smaller the longer it burns, but this is merely the "body" or vehicle by which the light is transmitted; the light itself remains constant. This is because light does not belong in the four levels of existence — inanimate, vegetative, animate and human — but is, like electricity, a force and a source of energy. As such it has a very close affinity to pure metaphysical energy, which in turn gives us an insight into the importance of light in ritual and celebration.

To summarizse, we can say that the concepts of goodness, beneficence, positive energy, the Desire to Impart, light, all-inclusiveness, total fulfillment and the lack of the Desire to Receive, are all manifestations of one single concept, all interlocking and inseparable, and comprising in their totality the nature of the Creator.

The Kabbalah teaches us that the first state of existence of which we can have any knowledge is the *En Sof,* the Endless World. As its name implies, this state is without beginning or end, and within it there are no manifestations of the concepts of time, space or motion. Thus when we talk of events taking place within the *En Sof* we should always bear in mind that these are merely distinctions we impose, and not discrete operations within the endless World. It is only through the separation of existence into the modes of time, space and motion that we can bring our limited powers of understanding to bear on a problem, but the unfolding of the process of Creation in the *En Sof* is governed purely and solely by cause and effect, with no discernible extention or movement. The Ari says of this stage of Creation that "There were no distinguishable or discernible levels or grades."[46] The modes of thought and perception by which we attempt to understand the external world only came into being after the process of Creation was finished, as we shall see.

Yesh Ma'ayin

We have said that the creator's attribute is sharing or imparting; however, there can be no sharing unless there is some agent that can receive. We should also note that the Creator's infinite desire to impart implies a desire to fulfill every possible grade and quality of desires to receive: whether there was a desire for health, wisdom, money or possessions, its fulfillment was contained in the original desire to impart.

Here we have what the Kabbalah calls the Thought of Creation, the process by which G-d's infinite desire to impart led to the creation of a vessel to receive His blessings. Although we talk of 'a vessel' (or *Sefira*), we must remember that, due to the infinite desire to impart, the vessel must also be considerd in the aspect of an infinite number of vessels, each receiving its individual fulfillment from the Creator. The creation of this vessel according to the Kabbalah, was the beginning and the end of Creation.

If all that existed was the desire to impart, then all that was created was the desire to receive. The desire to impart could not have been created itself, for the process of creation implies that something previously non-existent has been brought into existence; yet we have already stated that the essence of the desire to impart is that it is full and lacks nothing. It is therefore inconceivable that the desire to impart itself should be created, since lacking nothing, existence must be one of its attributes. We find this explained in Nachmanides' commentary on the line from the morning prayer, "He forms the light, and He creates the darkness." The Ramban asks why two different words are used —

formed and created — and concludes that the light (which, as we have said, indicates the force of positive energy) could not be created, since creation indicates incompleteness, and the light is always whole. Instead, it was 'formed', meaning that it was moulded and circumscribed so that it could descend from the *En Sof.* The darkness, however, can be said to have been 'created', since darkness is an indication of incompleteness, of negative energy, and of the desire to receive. As such, it was not present in any form whatever within the Creator, but was created as a totally new phenomenon.

The creation of this vessel called the desire to receive is therefore called, *"Yesh ma'Ayin"*, meaning that something (*yesh*) was created from nothing (*ayin*). The nothing from which the desire to receive was created should under no circumstances be mistaken for such concepts as emptiness or blackness: it is simply a state of non- or pre-existence, devoid of any attribute.

We have now reached a stage in our description of the process of the Creation of the worlds where the actual essence of Creation has already taken place. The Kabbalah justifies its claim that the creation of the vessel of receiving, the *Yesh ma'Ayin,* was the whole of Creation on the grounds that all subsequent emanations and unfoldings are essentially no more than the multiplying results of this primal union of Cause (positive) and effect (negative).

It is precisely this mystical "nothingness" (*ayin*) from which all manifestations unfold, whether in terrestrial or celestial worlds: it is known in Kabbalah as the "hidden cause". But this "nothing" is in fact immeasurably more real than any other existence, since it is from this stage that the entire creation sprang. Creation from nothing actually typifies, and is the prime example of the process of emanation (which presupposes a source of emanation) and indeed the very creative process itself which, as we have mentioned, produces something new without involving the processes of logical thinking.

The relationship between the Creator, His beneficence and the

Sefirot, is comparable to that between the soul and the body, and between the essence and the vessel that contains it; but there is one difference, in that both the soul and the body differ in nature from the Creator. The soul, while symbolising the imparting aspect of the Creator, nevertheless has equal characteristic of the body — namely a Desire to Receive.

The idea of "nothingness" is not as complicated and mystical as it might seem at first sight: it is merely a convenient conceptual aid to encapsulate the idea of something that results from a thought, an effect that ensued after a prior motivating cause and which, having been non-existent, is considered as "something that emanated from nothingness". This idea is at the same time simple and profound: it states that there is no such thing as "nothingness", the world being made from the Eternal Substance of the Desire to Receive. The Creation of the world was the radical formation of this substance into what we know as our world.

This basic insight helps us to understand the paradoxes that permeate the entire Kabbalah. It deals with the world as it actually is, revealing the true immutable substance of the universe, as opposed to the changing appearance and transforming realities of the lower levels of existence. Only the underlying truth abides, the real substance of the universe, as opposed to the physical substance that we can touch but which decays and fades as the Light in it dies. Viewed in its simplest form, the Desire to Receive therefore signifies Creation in its totality. As a result of the Creator's original Desire to Impart, which was the motivating factor behind the Creation of the Desire to Receive, there arose a new phenomenon — the Desire to Receive, which is said to have sprung from "nothing" to indicate the elemental characteristic of the Creator.

However, there are still many stages of emanation before we can see the eventual emergence of our physical universe.

Shutting-off of the Light.

Let us return to the original Thought of Creation, which as we said was to share the Creator's boundless blessings. If we consider this concept of sharing, or imparting, we shall see that it makes certain demands on the recipient. We know from our own experience that the mere mechanical act of giving is, in itself, unsatisfactory. We do not give advice to the trees, nor do we offer money to animals. Clearly there must be a desire to receive on the part of the recipient, a knowledge of what the gift entails and signifies, before we can say that we are truly giving.

This is true for all levels of giving and receiving. There can be no sharing or imparting unless the recipient both knows and wants what he is being offered. Penetrating even more deeply into the nature of sharing and receiving, we find that these two criteria of knowledge and desire imply a previous possesion of that which is sought. Thus in a daydream we may possess our wildest hopes and fantasies, and taste the enjoyment of them just as though they were real; however, on waking, that pleasure fades away. We learn from this that our desires are constantly receiving fulfillment, but that the fulfillment is never permanent because we are unable to complete the circuit by sharing with others. Nonetheless, we can see that the subject of the desire to receive (the content of the dream) must be present before we can think of fulfilling it.

It also follows, however, that we must have lost what we possessed before we can desire it. Who desires food when he has enough to eat? Who desires wealth when he has all that money can buy? It is only after we have lost something that we can want it back; while we still possess it, that particular vessel or desire to receive is filled, and feels no sense of loss.

If the Thought of Creation was to create a desire to receive, as we have said, then the creation of the vessel in its initial form in the *En Sof* did not completely achieve this end. This vessel, which we referred to as *Yesh ma'Ayin,* is completely and everlastingly filled with Light and therefore cannot experience any desire to receive in itself. Indeed, its structure is indistinguishable from the Light, which is the desire to impart. The arousal of this desire to impart by the vessel is called the second stage of Creation — 'stage' being understood in the sense of cause and effect, not, we should remember, in terms of time.

There now exists a situation where the infinite number of vessels all desire to share with one another. This, however, is not possible because each is, at this stage, completely fulfilled. So sensitive are the vessels to one another's desire to share, however, that each one empties itself voluntarily of its light. This is the only way in which they can enable one another to share. We could compare this to a rich man deciding to get rid of all of his money so that he can provide other people with the opportunity of sharing their wealth with him. While he is in possession of his money, he has all that he wants, and consequently no desire to receive. It is only after he has made himself poor that he can enable others to share with him.

Now as soon as the vessel brings about this shutting-off, it becomes empty, and is referred to as the third stage. This emptiness brings about the fourth and final stage of Creation, for here we find the completion of the original Thought of Creation. Once the vessel becomes empty, it feels the lack of what was previously contained — the Light of Creation. Here then we find for the first time the criteria for the existence of the Desire to Receive.

This stage completes the world of Creation that is called the *En Sof*. In Rabbi Ashlag's commentary on the Tree of Life, we read:

"This last grade, in its complete perfection, is found only in the Endless World, before the creation of all the worlds."[47]

Rabbi Ashlag goes on to describe the next step in the emanation of the lower worlds: "The perfect will to receive of the Endless World underwent a restriction, or tsimtsum."[48]

This is explained as follows: since the desire to receive, which had been established in the *En Sof,* was now receiving the infinite beneficence of the Creator (fourth stage), there arose a feeling called Bread of Shame. The vessel is receiving continuously, but can do nothing in return inasmuch as the Creator, being whole and lacking nothing, has no desire to receive. The vessel feels Bread of Shame because it is unable to earn what it is receiving. Furthermore it is no longer merely a passive recipient as it was in the second stage of the *En Sof,* before the appearance of the Desire to Receive. Now it actively wants the light that it lost in the third stage of Creation, but cannot take it due to its inability to offer anything in return. The metaphysical energy generated by this situation brings about the restriction, or tsimtsum. It leads, by the principle of cause and effect, to a voluntary shutting-off of the Light, so that it can redress the existing lack of balance.

The resultant emptiness and lack of light gives birth to the infinite desires to receive of the physical world, in which we are placed in an incomplete state so that we can eliminate the Bread of Shame by sharing with others who are also lacking, and in this way fulfill our own desires.

This is the reason for placing an unfulfilled desire to receive in man. The original Thought of Creation was only to impart the Creator's infinite blessings, but we must first learn how to construct the link between giving and taking by means of *mitzvot* and precepts before we can bring that Thought to completion.

It should be noted that the arousal of Bread of Shame is very different from the arousal of the desire to impart in the *En Sof* or the emptying of the vessels. The concept of Bread of Shame only comes into existence after the evolution of the desire to receive, which was the last of the four stages of Creation in the *En Sof.*

"The restriction of Light occurred outside the Endless World, and, following this first restraint, the function of limiting became operative in all the worlds below it."[49]

Some might ask why this whole process is necessary: if the Creator is All-Powerful, as we have said, why could He not have created a vessel that would have a desire to receive without a desire to impart? Why was it necessary to bring us down to this mundane world of suffering and hardship? How can we, with our desire for the pleasures and luxuries of our physical exist-ence, ever hope to achieve re-unification with the Creator? The answer to these questions lies in a closer study of the Creation and a deeper understanding of the significance of the teachings of Kabbalah. To those who have understood the explanation given here, it should be clear that the intention of the Creator was only to do good, this being His very nature. The restriction and emptying of the vessel in the fourth stage of Creation, how-ever, was a voluntary act brought about by the vessel itself. The laws regarding the flow and transfer of metaphysical energy, from which all physical manifestations grow, were established from the beginning of Creation and are an expression of the attributes of the Creator. However, what is established by volun-tary means on a high level becomes involuntary on successively lower levels. This is similar to a law which is established volun-tarily by a process of debate and decision in the governing body of a state or country and which subsequently becomes binding on all the citizens over whom the jurisdiction extends.

The essential laws regarding the flow of energy in the universe were therefore established in the process of Creation. These laws include the reasons why we are present on this physical world, and why we are subject to the desires that we experience. Unfor-tunately, we are prone to forget that which was voluntary in the *En Sof* becomes involuntary in our universe. The freedom that our souls chose voluntarily by restricting the light of the *En Sof* was intended to give us the opportunity to redress the balance between what we were receiving and what we could impart to others. Nonetheless that freedom is still subject to the higher laws of Creation. While we can now exercise our desire to receive for our own gratification, without any thought of sharing with others, the essential structure of the universe (Bread of Shame, restriction) still applies. Gratification, whether it be spir-itual or physical, will still last only if there is a balance between receiving and sharing.

This should answer the often-asked question regarding free will. Why could the Creator not merely have commanded us to obey the laws and precepts, instead of leaving us with such a confusing amount of choice? From what we have already said regarding the evolution of the universe, it should be clear that the decision not to receive was ours and ours alone. It was taken because of the imbalance that existed, and it was taken with the sole purpose of restoring balance. If the Creator were to order us to receive His infinite blessings, we would be faced with the same unacceptable imbalance that brought about the original feeling of Bread of Shame, which would in turn bring about a restriction, returning us full circle to our present state. Clearly, our first concern should be to eliminate the feeling of Bread of Shame, for this is the cause of the restriction that cuts us off from the light. Furthermore, it is as a direct result of the restriction that was brought about by the vessel of receiving that the forces of evil became manifest in our universe. Until there was a lack or emptiness there could be no evil, since the nature of evil is the unfulfilled desire to receive. If we examine our desires for the physical benefits of this world, we find that they all stem from this same root — the lack of fulfillment. Whether our desire is for money, status or possessions, the common element is always the desire to receive, an awareness that we have lost a fulfillment we once had and can regain it by amassing physical objects. We have lost sight of the true purpose of our existence on this physical level that the desire to receive has become more real to us than the Light, which is the desire to impart. In showing us the forces by which the universe was created, the Zohar provides us with the reasons for our existence, and indicates unequivocally the work we have to accomplish during our brief period of existence on this world.

The question of purpose is discussed by the sages of the Zohar who provide the simple answer that He might bestow upon it His infinite love and abundance. The thought behind Creation was to share with mankind. The effect of this motivating cause was the creation of man as a vessel for that bestowal, thus revealing the true essence of man as the Desire to Receive. Without this Desire to Receive, the creation of the world could not have proceeded, since the concept of positive energy must, out of necessity, come before the concept of negative energy; one could not possibly desire something without the prior capacity to desire.

Consequently we cannot speak of Creation when referring to the Light, which would designate something newly-made or newly-revealed. Creation refers not to the Light but to the newly revealed phenomenon of the Desire to Receive. Within this concept alone were contained all future manifestations of Creation, including the physical world together with its central point, man.

At the time of the revelation of Creation, the Desire to Receive was like the seed of a tree. A tree is made up of roots, trunk, branches and leaves, all evolving indisputably from the seed, yet not discernable to the naked eye while contained within it: the seed gives no sign of its future development into a tree. Through a series of evolutions, man developed from his root or seed, which was the original revelation of the Desire to Receive. As man appears in our world, he is but an emanation or evolution of that Desire. His inner, hidden essence remains the Desire to Receive.

Now it should be clearly understood that this Desire to Receive is not necessarily degrading, nor is it to be considered a liability. On the contrary, as we have seen, it is the vital pivot of Creation. We can modify our Desire to Receive and channel its demands into areas that will strengthen us and draw us nearer to the Light, but we can never destroy it. This is in absolute opposition to those religions that claim man's objective to be the removal or destruction of the ego. According to the Kabbalah, this feat is only accomplished after the death of the body.

Only through a complete understanding of the Desire to Receive in all its manifestations will we come to a better understanding of our inner motivating consciousness and its relationship with our physical actions, and far more importantly, a better understanding of our relationship with our fellow-men. All this information is provided for us by the *Zohar*. The Zohar shows us the sublime wisdom concerning the metaphysical characteristics of all Creation, which is the Desire to Receive.

CHAPTER IX

THE MAJOR CONCEPTS

Not all the concepts of Kabbalah are susceptible to direct description. Much of the analysis of upper and lower worlds is carried out through analogy and metaphor. Through the use of colourful images, an imaginative link is established between the phenomena being described and the tangible world in which we live; otherwise the world described by Kabbalah would remain forever closed and inaccessible. The imagery enables us to discern the reality and helps us understand more surely the consequences that flow from the inner meaning of the image.

It is for this reason that the analysis of the concept of *Yesh Ma-ayin* is central to the understanding of the purpose of this imagery. We must imagine a world, spiritual in content, which lies beyond the immediate grasp of the senses. It is a world that exists both within and beyond our physical existence, with its own structure, modes of behaviour, patterns of identity and communications; it sees without being seen. This metaphysical realm bears the same relation to the sensible world as the Creator does to the Creation, or the soul to the body. The implication of this analogy is that, in order for the transcendant to be known, it must assume the guise of the material. This has obvious echoes of the concept of *Yesh Ma-ayin,* but, whereas *Yesh Ma-ayin* is a general description of the process of the Creation, Kabbalah in its wider applications also deals with the realities of our physical existence, whether as individuals or as a people.

The most common metaphor used for describing this progress from higher to lower spiritual levels involves the image of Light, the content, and the vessel, the container. These exist on all levels, whether we are dealing with different types of spiritual worlds (*olamot*), their constituent parts (*sefirot*), or with the major process by which one level is transformed into the next. The configuration of light and vessel at any particular stage in their development is called *partzuf* (face or countenance). At the very beginning of this process, is a cosmic event known as 'the breaking of the vessels' (*shevirat hekelim*) were the initial vessels through which the creation is to be formed and shaped are unable to contain the power of the spiritual light which pours into them, and shatter. Here, too, we have a warning to future generations not to run before they can walk in spiritual matters.

The result of this cosmic explosion necessitates the formation of far more sturdy vessels which will be able to contain the light. By virtue of their thickness, however, vessels tend to hide the light they contain, and for which they are meant to act as conduits. In the final stage, where the vessels are co-terminuous with the tangible world of the senses, the light is practically invisible.

Yet the very dynamism by which this process operates also contains within itself its own purpose. The creator veils his *Or Ein Sof* (Eternal Light) in order to allow this world to exist in its present form. This should not be understood to mean that Creation is separated from the Creator — Heaven forbid — but rather that the spiritual end-product of Creation — man — has the facility within himself to uncover the source and purpose of his own creation. This is to be achieved specifically through the tools of study, prayer and *Mitzvot,* the end goal of which is called *Devekut,* the attachment of man to his Creator, the re-unification of all vessels and lights.

Let us now examine these concepts in greater detail.

Giving and Taking — The Purpose of our Existence.

The purpose of Creation, as we have said, was to impart boundless goodness to all. The existence of an inherent Desire to Receive was also explained as the expression of one of the profound truths by which the Creation was revealed. This Desire to Receive constitutes the vessel, indicating the exact measure of the bounty to be received, since the dimensions of the Light (forces of goodness) are in exact proportion to the Desire to Receive. The Creator in His wisdom imparts to a spiritual, metaphysical entity no more and no less than is desired, if He were to impart more light than the vessel desired or required, this would in essence contradict the very nature of His infinite love and abundance, for there can be no degree of spiritual coercion in His goodness. To impart or share with others, on any level ,can only be considered noble and kind when the recipient desires and enjoys that which is offered to him. However, when the recipient rejects the gift yet the donor continues to insist on its acceptance, one can hardly consider this an act of giving, since the response and pleasure of giving lie in the joy of receiving. There can be little true satisfaction to either party in a gift that is neither sought nor desired, and which is consequently misused or discarded.

It follows from this that G-d's beneficence cannot manifest itself or prevail without an active Desire to Receive on the part of man, despite His omnipotence which permits Him to demand and exact our obedience. This sublime idea is emphasized with striking clarity by Rabbi Shimon: "no influence from above can prevail unless it is preceded by a stimulus from below."[50] The symmetry and harmony between these opposing forces, whether we talk of them as positive and negative or cause and effect, is necessary for the continuous and uninterrupted flow of energy.

This law is ultimately linked with the question of the fundamental purpose behind the giving of the Torah, with its precepts and commandments. The Zohar states, "since the Creator has the attribute of all-goodness, He therefore created this mundane world with its human inhabitants. Thus the Creator could now bestow upon them His infinite love and abundance.

"However, should all this be true," continues the Zohar, "if G-d indeed desired to bestow His abundance upon humanity, then why did He cast the noble and divine souls to this earthly, sublunar plane, into bodies built of clay, where they endure sorrow, temptation and the constant trials of the demonic forces of hatred and ruthlessness which the material body imposes on the soul? He might, preferably, have maintained them in His Heavenly sphere where all spirits rejoice in Paradise, where they merit the ineffable goodness of the Divine splendour which is bestowed upon them." The reason, according to the Zohar, is that the world was created for man with all its blessings and problems. G-d created this world peopling it with earthly bodies through which the soul must labour and struggle. By prayer and study of Torah we can attain His objective of purification and sanctity; without the struggle this necessitates, we would be nothing more than an idle recipient of G-d's blessing.

"The natural consequence of eating unearned bread, of receiving something that is not earned by labour and endeavour," declares the Zohar, "is embarrassment and shame! he eats the Bread of Shame."[51]

Rabbi Shimon teaches us that in order to permit us to eliminate this feeling G-d provided us with the means of performing service to Him so that He might bestow His ineffable Heavenly Light upon purified souls while they are still on this earthly abode. Man thus eliminates all feeling of shame. Upon receiving the Light, the soul experiences the all-goodness and perfection of its Creator and recognises the delight and contentment which follow the successful implementation of exacting labour.

In the Zohar's view, the labour and service one exerts in the study of Torah and in the performance of *Mitzvot* is commensurate with the Heavenly bounty that one is granted. In fulfilling the precepts of the Creator with love and understanding, one is exerting one's Desire to Impart, and thus removing the bread of shame that prevents the boundless and eternal Light from entering the soul.

Reflection on the conclusion of the Zohar that "a lifetime of study of Torah, together with performance of its doctrines, equates with the reward of eternal happiness", leads to the question of whether it is possible to earn perpetual bliss with a mixture of corporeal and Divine servitude. We might compare this to a man engaged in manual labour for an hour a day for which he receives an enormous amount of money, far in excess of the value of the job. According to the Zohar, inequality of labour and reward, wherever it occurs, results in the aspect of bread of shame and leads to the sublime doctrine known as *tsimtsum,* or restriction.

Tsimtsum is the refusal of the Desire to Receive actually to receive, when to do so would cause an unacceptable imbalance. We would compare its operation to an overload switch in an electrical circuit which shuts off the power input when it exceeds a certain level, that level being dictated by the ability of the circuit to pass on, or share, the current. In the same way, an increasing metaphysical imbalance (bread of shame), where the soul is receiving more Light than it can cope with, leads to a restriction of that Light. *Tsimtsum* is the essential principle through which the Zohar traces the entire need for and process of Creation, with its manifold levels of celestial and terrestrial existence.

The Creator's purpose in creating the universe is, as we have said, to bestow his limitless goodness on humanity, and to share with the soul of man the newly-revealed phenomenon of the Desire to Receive. The spiritual substance that emanates from Him is called the Light of the *En Sof (Or En Sof)* or the Light of the Endless. Its essential characteristic is that it contains the potential of completely satisfying any Desire to Receive by providing its necessary fulfillment. This beneficence flows incessantly, comprising all the varied forms of spiritual nourishment and displaying an infinite degree of Heavenly bliss. It follows from this that innumerable phases of the Desire to Receive ensued as a result of the original thought of the Creator, each receiving fulfillment from the corresponding degree of bestowal.

Consequently, the first and primary world, which includes our own highly diverse universe, was included in the boundless, integrated, infinite and endless world known as the *Olam En Sof,* the world of the endless.[52]

This phase of Creation is shrouded in mystery and remains beyond the grasp of human conception and understanding. In it, we find the co-existence of the Desires to Impart and to Receive, representing together a simple and absolute unity that transcends material expression and the limits of time, space and motion in its diverse and multi-faceted form. This state might be compared to the seed, which contains all future manifestations in potential form, but which remains in complete unity at its source. Only when it begins to unfold and become subject to temporal and physical limitations do the elemental differences of the seed reveal themselves as separate entities — root, trunk, branch, and leaf.

When the exalted light of the *En Sof,* the Desire to Impart, the positive or causative factor, had completely and perfectly filled all existence, the Desire to Receive emerged within the world of the Endless. As a result of its emergence, no soul remained unfulfilled in its respective Desire to Receive-no soul required additional correction or perfection. This was eternal bliss at the pinnacle of its glory. The souls bore no trace of defect, lack or inferiority, no jealousy or hatred of one another, since each received complete and instant fulfillment from the Light of the Endless.

Out of His great love of sharing — a boundless love — comes the essence of the Creator who ceaselessly bestows His beneficence, the symbol of His divine perfection, the Desire to Impart, in which lies the root of His endless bliss.

The Doctrine of Tsimtsum and the Jewish People

The ultimate aim of G-d's creation is to benefit His creatures, so that even after the Creation, His radiance permeates the universe, as we read in the words of the Prophet Isaiah: "The whole world is filled with His Glory."[53] Yet how can we substantiate such a conviction? More particularly, how is it possible to maintain that such universal beneficence exists in relation to the one people for whom it is meant to have a special significance and purpose?

The logic of the Kabbalah would seem to imply that the Jewish people, more than any other, will bathe in the glory of the Creator's beneficence; are they not called the 'chosen people'? But the evidence of history shows quite a different picture. Jewish history is soaked with the blood of martyrdom, continuous affliction and punishment, intolerable sufferings, despairing hearts and languishing unhappiness. Yet even while enduring the bitter pain and humiliation of exile the Jews were expected to remain true to their faith throughout.

Our understanding of the woes that have befallen Jewry since time immemorial is made easier by the doctrine of *Tsimtsum,* the contraction of the Divine Light. The restriction, according to the Lurianic system, was executed as a voluntary restraint by the Desire to Receive because "there had arisen in His pure will the intention to create the worlds."[54] This means that, within the Kingdom of the *En Sof* which is the Desire to Receive, there was an aspiration towards achieving equality with the Infinite Light of the *En Sof,* which is the Desire to Impart. This was made possible and was destined to be revealed through the creation and existence of our universe. The yearning to be identified with the aspect of sharing, or imparting, which corresponds to the essence of the Infinite, grew out of the aspect of bread of shame; this, in turn, resulted from the continual receiving of the Kingdom of the *En Sof* from the endless Light. The result of these two stages was the rejection or restriction of the Light which created a vacuum; this vacuum, in turn, permitted the emanation and creation of all the worlds through the process of progressive revelation.

This vacuum of limitation, which is indicative of the unfulfilled

Desire to Receive, gave birth to primordial space and to the limitations of time, space and motion. Prior to the *Tsimtsum* (restriction), there had been no destructive influences at work in the universe, since there had been no desires left unfulfilled. However, due to the aspect of Bread of Shame brought about by the inability of the souls to earn the Light or to share their blessing with one another, they caused the Restriction. This, in turn, created the physical universe, which is governed by the laws of Restriction. This area of incompleteness and deficiency brought about by the self-imposed restriction of the Light ultimately leads to the chaos and lack of harmony that is called the Evil Inclination. Just as the physical veiling or screening of the light of the sun blocks its penetration, so the whole of Creation constitutes an enormous process of restriction or rejection brought about by the original *Tsimtsum* that took place in the World of the Infinite.

The involuntary restriction imposed upon man is due to the nature of the soul which is transformed on leaving its domain in the upper world so that it can live inside a body of flesh and blood. In the higher worlds, the soul experiences both the beneficence of the *En Sof* and the feeling of shame that is a result of the inability to impart anything to the all-inclusive Infinite. Thus the soul descends to this world in order to erase the feeling of shame and thereby achieves fulfillment. However, in passing into this world the soul forgets its purpose in coming here, due to the influence of the Evil Inclination, and becomes distracted by the earthly delights of this mundane existence.

In this connection, the story is told of a poor man who found himself unable to support his family . One day, a friend told of an island so far away that it took six months to reach, where diamonds were said to be so plentiful that he would be able to bring back enough to last him a lifetime. After consulting with his family, he decided that the difficulties of the journey and the pain of separation from those he loved would be amply compensated for by the rewards he could bring back, and so he embarked on a boat bound for the wonderful island.

When the boat eventually landed, he found that his friend's report had been true: diamonds lay in great heaps wherever he looked. Quickly he set about filling pockets, bags and boxes with the precious stones, but he was interrupted by a man who informed him that there was no need to make such haste, since the boat was not due to return to his homeland for another six months. It now became clear to the traveller that he would have to find some means of earning a living during these six months since the diamonds he had collected, being so common were of no value in this land. He made several enquiries and discovered that wax was a rare and precious commodity here, and that a man with the patience and skill to make candles would surely flourish.

Sure enough, he was soon proficient in candle-making, and earned enough for a good and comfortable life on the island, only occasionally thinking with sorrow of the family he had left behind. When the time came to leave after six months, he packed a case full of his precious candles and set off for his homeland. When he reached his native shores he was greeted rapturously by his friends and family and proudly displayed the fruits of his labour — a pile of worthless candles.

So it is with the souls who descend into this world to correct the imbalance of receiving and sharing through the conditioning agent of the Torah, but who neglect this Divine purpose and become preoccupied with the concerns of the body and of this transient world.

Most people are involved only on the physical level of existence, with its everchanging environment of effects and movement. It is easy to see how the apparently varied and complex interactions of the physical world could distract the soul from its true purpose, just as the poor man was distracted from his true purpose by the necessity of earning a living. However in order to maintain a balance between taking and sharing, the concept of restriction became an integral part of our organic mechanisms.

Thus in the process of receiving without having merited or earned the benefit, all the involuntary mechanisms intimately connected with our psyche become operative.

In every country where they are permitted to settle, Jews provide the mainstay of business, science and the arts. Their success in almost any venture to which they turn is an indication of their strong Desire to Receive — the most powerful of any nation. However, if there is not also an awareness of the importance of balancing this Desire to Receive with an equally great Desire to Impart, the Jew will find that all he has to show for his time on earth is the "wax" of a selfish and self-centered existence.

Through his limitless Desire to Receive he can create potent forces of negative energy, causing the Creator to turn his face away from the Jewish people as a father chastises his favourite son. If these negative energies created by the imbalance of the Desire to Receive are allowed to build up, the Angel of Death is given access to the Jews, and his power reigns over them until they eliminate the negativity by balancing the Desire to Receive with one of Imparting, through the medium of the commandments and mitzvot contained in the Torah.

For one to capture and retain permanent spiritual nourishment or emotional satisfaction, the interaction of giving must at all times be balanced, thus enabling the Light of all-inclusive beneficence perpetually to illuminate each and every corner of our being.

We see this process at work every second of our lives, in the mechanism by which we draw the breath of life into our lungs and then expel it. The drawing-in represents the Desire to Receive, the exhaling of air the Desire to Impart; clearly the two must be in perfect balance at all times. We also notice that we must breathe in before we can breathe out, just as we must have a Desire to Receive before we can share, and we cannot exhale a greater amount of air than we breathe in. Thus the metaphysical symbol of restriction reflects a highly developed conception of the cosmological process and drama of attraction and repulsion, a drama in which the Divine scheme of man's place and function is revealed as corresponding completely to the original *Tsimtsum.*

The phase of receptivity, which forms one part of this dualism, is on a par with the Supreme Light of the Emanator and enables the created being — man to join with the Creator in perfect union. The totality of these metaphysical forces forms a balanced and harmonious structure which is made manifest by the enveloping of the Light by the vessel of the Desire to Receive. As long as the relationship remains a directly symmetrical one, as in the *En Sof,* the objective of receiving fulfillment of a permanent nature can be achieved.

The Desire to Receive which, as we have seen, was originally created for the sole purpose of drawing down the endless blessings of the Creator, is all too often transformed on our physical level of existence into a Desire to Receive for the body alone, without any thought of sharing. A great Desire to Receive is not, in itself, harmful in that it contains within it the constant opportunity of an equally large desire to Share. It is only when the Desire to Receive dominates the individual, so that it is no longer subject to any restraint, that inbalance occurs and the individual, by his selfish acts and thoughts, cuts himself off from the Creator and from the source of spiritual nourishment. What we find under such circumstances is an increasingly desperate pursuit of pleasure and satisfaction; without the lasting aspect of the union of upper and lower worlds which comes from an awareness of the circular concept of receiving and sharing, only the vessels of pleasure are left, without the Light that is pure and everlasting joy. This is the meaning of the sages when they wrote, "He who desires money will not be satisfied with money": in all our feverish pursuit of the good things in this life, we are apt to forget that these are merely the outward forms, or vessels, of pleasure! Even if we have earned them, by the standards of this world, the pleasure they contain is small and transient when compared to the enduring beneficence of the Creator that is constantly accessible to us through the Torah and its precepts, which act as a restraint and a channelling of our Desire to Receive.

The Chosen People

It is hard for the contemporary Jew to come to terms with his role as one of the Chosen People. The term Chosen begs so many questions, few of which are answered satisfactorily by traditional sources of learning. By whom were we chosen, and from whom? Why were we chosen and for what task? Is that task the same today as it was when Moses received the Law on Mount Sinai? How can we fulfill that task today, given the apparent difference in circumstances between our time and the time of the Exodus? It is only when we turn to Kabbalah that we begin to understand the reason for this expression — the Chosen people — and its implications for Jews throughout the ages.

We must start by understanding the significance of the Patriarch Abraham, who is called the Chariot of Hesed (Mercy). Through his spiritual attributes Abraham was the vehicle by means of which the potential energy that is called Hesed (Mercy) was brought down to this earth. However, to penetrate more deeply into the meaning of this concept, it will help to study the Torah's description of the Creation.

"In the beginning, G-d created the heaven and the earth... And G-d called the light Day, and the darkness He called Night. And the evening and the morning were one day... And G-d called the firmament Heaven. And the evening and the morning were the second day... And G-d said, Let be there lights in the firmament of the heaven to divide the day from the night..."[55]

The first question we have to ask is why there appears to be so much repetition in this description; we are told, for instance, that Heaven was created on the second day, yet it is also referred to in the first verse, where we are told that it was created on the first day. In the same way we learn that day and night were established on the first day, yet the process seems to be repeated on the fourth day, when the lights came into being to distinguish day from night. Another strange feature of this passage is that the first day is called *"yom ehad"*, meaning "day one", as opposed to all the subsequent days which are called the second, third, fourth, etc.

These problems begin to unravel themselves only when we recall that the essence of Creation is the progressive transformation of energy levels, which are known as the Sefirots. Now we know that this process of transformation does not alter the root of the energy at all; it merely reveals a different aspect of the energy, just as when water is poured into a number of different coloured glasses, we see a different colour in each glass, but know that the water has not been altered. The sefirot or vessels, operate in the same way, diversifying the original energy of the *En Sof*. On the first day of Creation, the energy level of *Hesed* was brought into being; However, this *sefira* represents a complete unified whole, like the seed that contains within itself the potential for all future growth and manifestation. This is why the Torah refers to the first day as *"yom ehad"* (one day), stressing its undifferentiated aspect compared to the following days. We can also see now why the differentiation of heaven and earth, and of day and night, are mentioned as having taken place on *"yom ehad"* as well as on the second and fourth days; the *sefira* of *Hesed* contains all these elements, but they do not appear as separate entities until further transformations have taken palce.

Let us now return to Abraham who, as we said, represents the *sefira* of *Hesed*. It is in him that the unique spiritual structure of the Jews has its beginning, just as all the manifestations of the Creation had their beginning in that unified day of *Hesed*. The structure is still only in potential form at this stage, needing to progress through successive transformations before it can become implanted into individual souls on the occasion of the giving of the Law on Mount Sinai. It can be compared to a seed that has been planted in the ground — no longer just a potential for growth, as it was before it was planted, but still keeping the same structure of that seed, and not yet showing any form of change or attachment to the earth. Thus we can say that in relation to previous states, the energy of *Hesed* is brought down onto the physical level by Abraham, while in terms of subsequent transformations, it still remains in the metaphysical realms of potential. . .

The next step in the revelation of the meaning of "the Chosen People" comes in the inheritance that Abraham gives to his son, Isaac:

"And Abraham gave all that he had unto Isaac. But unto the sons of the concubines which Abraham had, Abraham gave gifts, and sent them away from Isaac his son, while he yet lived, eastward, unto the east country."[56]

The Zohar here explains that "Abraham transmitted to Isaac the exalted doctrine of the true faith, so that he should be joined to his proper grade."[57] It goes on to discuss the gifts that were given to the sons of the concubines: "What sort of gifts were they? They comprised the sides of the low grades, which are the names of the powers of the unclean spirit, so as to complete the whole list of grades."[58]

Isaac's inheritance was therefore the knowledge of the secrets of the structure of the metaphysical world, so as to permit him to connect with the upper world. Without this knowledge of the upper world, Isaac would not have been able to establish his ordained link with the *sefira* or *Gevurah* (judgement), of which he is the chariot.

The knowledge that was given to Isaac, we must remember, is still in a state of concealment; it is not something that can be passed on among the Jewish people but must be transmitted only to the next level of transformation, which is the chariot of Isaac. Hence the Zohar asks, "What sort of gifts were they?" If the total system in embryo was given to Isaac, what was left to give the other sons? It replies that these were lower levels of understanding. An incomplete system, since the complete system which is the system of three columns, had not yet been revealed. Because the sons of the concubines took away an incomplete system by which to govern their lives, it is called 'unclean' (*tumah*), or incomplete. According to the Zohar, this is the origin of the various eastern religions which seek to amend their lack of a central column by denying the merit of the left column, which is the desire to receive:

It is written, 'And Solomon's wisdom excelled the wisdom of all the children of the east.' (I Kings V, 10). This is an allusion to the descendants of the children of Abraham's concubines who, as we have already said, live in the mountains of the east, where they instruct the sons of men in the arts of magic and divination.[59]

Thus we see that the knowledge of the complete system of three columns was passed from Abraham to Isaac. But knowledge itself is not sufficient — these must also be tools with which to put that knowledge into practice. The culmination of this gradual unfolding and revealing of the system came with the exodus from Egypt, followed fifty days later by the giving of the Law on Mount Sinai, which we commemorate by the festival of *Shavuoth*. It is on this occasion that we are given a direct indication of the meaning of the Chosen People.

"And Moses went up unto G-d, and the Lord called unto Him out of the mountain saying, 'Thus shalt thou say to the house of Jacob, and tell the children of Israel; Ye have seen what I did unto the Egyptians, and how I bore you on eagles' wings, and brought you unto myself. Now, therefore, if you will obey my voice indeed, and keep my convenant, then you shall be a special treasure unto me above all people: for all the earth is mine."[60]

With Abraham we saw the concept of the three columns contained within the context of *Hesed*, which is positive energy; with Isaac the system evolves within the framework of *Gevurah* (judgment), which is negative energy; Jacob finally brings the system into its appointed place, which is the energy of the central

—97—

column (Jacob being the chariot of *Tiferet*, beauty). However, the children of Israel themselves must be aware of the system before they can be said to have freely accepted it. This is the significance of the passage quoted above ("Ye have seen..."). When they put the blood on their doorposts in Egypt to ward off the Angel of Death, they were witnessing the operation of an elevated and potent system of laws. That same system, in its entirety, was to be presented to them on Mount Sinai. Having had the basic structure of the Law implanted in them by the Chariots of the Patriarchs, the Jews were now ready to be presented with the 'operational tools' of Torah.

The Zohar tells us that, although they were thus primed for the knowledge of Torah, it was nevertheless first offered to the other nations, who rejected it!

"It is written, 'Lord, when thou went forth out of Seir, when Thou marched out of the field of Edom, the earth trembled.'[61] This refers to the fact that, before G-d gave the Law to Israel, He offered it to the children of Esau and to the children of Ishmael, but they would not accept it."[62]

The text of the Zohar goes on to relate the reasons for this, telling us why the other nations refused the Torah.

"He therefore summoned Samael (the ministering angel of Esau) and said to him, 'Do you desire my law?' 'What is written in it?' he asked. The Lord replied, using a passage to test him, 'Thou shalt not kill.' Then Samael said, 'Heaven save us. This Torah is thine, and let it remain thine. I do not want it... If thou givest it to me, all my dominion will disappear, for it is based on slaughter and on the planet of Mars; if there are no wars, my power will pass away from the world."[63]

Samael recommends that the Law be given to "the sons of Jacob", thinking that the restrictions of Torah would eliminate their power. In the same way, the Torah is offered to Rahab (the angel with influence over Ishmael), who rejects the Law on the grounds that his dominion is based on the sexual urge expressed in the blessing given to Adam in the Garden of Eden, "Be fruitful and multiply" (Gen. 8:17). Since the Torah forbids adultery, Rahab fears that it will deprive him of the source of his power.

It should be noted that on each of these occasions the offer is made not to the people themselves, but to the angel who presides over their destiny:

"He summoned all the myriads of holiness who are appointed to rule over the other nations, and they gave Him the same reply."[64]

It is only in the case of the children of Israel that the entire population is brought together and prepared to accept the Law. This tells us something about the special nature of the attachment between Israel and G-d. The other nations are ruled by prevailing influences, by the instincts that are indicated by the angels, while Israel has chosen to bind itself to the Almighty Himself. This binding is symbolised by the binding of Isaac, indicating the restricting power of the central column. This is also symbolised by the precept of *Tefillin*, and by the passage already mentioned, "You shall be a special treasure unto me above all people."

To the other nations of the world, Judaism appears to be a fiercely prohibitive religion. The Angel Samael believed that its restrictive force would crush it out of existence. However, for the Jew, with his unique metaphysical structure, the Torah enables him to elevate every aspect of his existence to the same exalted level that is represented by the lives of the Patriarchs.

The Zohar tells us that G-d was "like a physician who had a phial of some elixir which he wanted to keep for his son. He was a clever man, and he said to himself, 'I have bad servants in my house; if they learn of my intention to give my son this present, they will be jealous of him and try to kill him. So what did he do? He took a little poison and smeared it round the edge of the phial. Then he summoned his servants and said to them, You are faithful servants; do you want to try some of this drug? They said, Let us see what it is. They tasted a small amount and had hardly smelt it before they came near to death. They said to themselves, if he gives this poison to his son, he will surely die and we shall gain his inheritance. They therefore said to him, Master, this drug has been merited only by your son... So G-d, being a wise physician, knew that if He gave the Torah to Israel without telling (the other nations), they would every day pursue them and kill them for it."[65]

Just as the faith of the children of Israel when they were slaves in Egypt enabled them to overcome the opposition of the prevailing influence of that country, which was the left column, the desire to receive, so adherence to the precepts of Torah will help them to rise above the predominant influences of Esau and Ishmael. The implications contained in this passage for contemporary Judaism and its status in the world need little amplification.

We have stated earlier that what was voluntary in the upper worlds becomes involuntary in the lower; having chosen the Law on Mount Sinai, we bound ourselves forever to that system of operation, knowing it to be our true salvation. If we choose to neglect it, then we once more enter the realm of the lower worlds, with their incomplete structures and influences. The choice presented to us, and open to us at every moment, is between the instant gratification that follows the fulfillment of the desire to receive if there is no restriction or sharing and the eternal and never-ending blessing that comes from a system that is functioning at all times in accord and harmony with the structure of the upper world. The difference may be expressed as the contrast between a contact and a connection. The first allows only momentary flow of energy, which is why physical pleasures are called instant, or transitory. The second, however, permits the existence of a permanent channel for the flow of energy from the upper worlds. The energy here can be passed on via the channels, so that it does not build up in the system and cause a shutting-off. This is why the reward for adherence to Spiritual Judaism is timeless and infinite.

The word used for Chosen in Torah is *segulah*, from the same root as the vowel *segol*, which is shown as three points. This

should remind us of the three columns that comprise the structure of Torah, and of all Jews. On Mount Sinai, where the souls
of all Jews were present, we were shown how to live within the
framework of these three columns — how to organise our lives
so as to connect with these three forces. In this way the energy
represented by the Torah was established and connected for all
time to this universe by the presence of the Jewish people and
their exodus from Egypt. Our heritage, therefore, is to channel
these energies constructively, avoiding and eliminating clashes
and disruptions in the world, in order to bring about the reign of
peace and harmony for all peoples. Nor should this role be
understood as implying the need for active intervention, any
more than the children of Israel intervened actively in their
deliverance from Egypt. The structure of the three columns that
they established by putting blood on the two doorposts and the
lintel, which indicated that they were acting within that framework, was sufficient in itself to raise them above the harmful
influences that had enslaved them. In the same way, knowledge
of the paths and laws of energy that are given to us in Torah is
sufficient to enable us to fulfill our purpose in this physical
world.

The nature of all the forces of uncleanliness and impurity is the
left column, the desire to receive for oneself alone. The essential
characteristic of the desire to receive is lack of fulfillment. It is
therefore not necessary to battle with these forces directly. It is
possible to resolve conflicts at their source, rather than having to
wait for them to manifest themselves through the workings of
time, space and motion. Thus "you have seen what I did unto the
Egyptians,"[66] by an action that did nothing more than draw down
a particular form of energy, the desired effect on the physical
realm was brought about.

We have given some indication here of the ways in which the
Zohar throws light on the expression 'the Chosen People', show-
ing how the concept of the three columns emerged through the
Patriarchs, to be established finally on the occasion of the giving

of the Law. It is in the completeness of this system, compared with the limited method of left and right columns only that were given to the 'sons of the concubines of Abraham', that we find the true significance of our role as the Chosen People.

The *sefirot*, or vessels, are the system used in Kabbalah to describe the process by which the unified energy of the *En Sof* is diversified in its transmission from the upper world to the lower levels. Each *sefira* represents a different form of what we might call "bottled-up energy", with different characteristics and attributes.

Sefirot

The concept of the *sefirot* has many and wide-ranging implications in the teachings of Kabbalah. The purpose of this section is only to introduce the reader in a general way to the system of *sefirot*, so that he will become aware of their occurrence and significance in subsequent studies. The simplest way to begin to understand the *sefirot* is through the patriarchs. Each represents a certain form of energy which is characteristic of one of the *sefirot*, and is the Chariot, or vehicle, by means of which that particular energy is brought down from its potential form in the metaphysical realm into an active form in our universe. Thus by studying the stories told in the Torah about the patriarchs, we can obtain a closer understanding of the sort of energy indicated by each of the *sefirot*.

The first three *sefirot* are the means by which Light was brought into this world; they are called *Keter* (crown), *Hochma (wisdom) and Bina* (intelligence). However since they do not in any way affect our physical world, other than by conducting the Light into it, they are considered a part of *Sitrei Torah* (q.v.) and will not be discussed here. Thus the first *sefira* that we shall consider is *Hesed* (mercy), which is the energy we associate with goodness and kind actions. The patriarch who brought down this energy was Avraham who, we are told, was always ready to welcome guests into his house; this is why the Talmud says that his home had four doors — it was never closed to anyone in need. When Avraham was circumcised and in great pain, we are told that G-d caused a period of unusually hot weather, so that people would stay at home instead of disturbing Avraham's rest and recovery.[67] The energy of *Hesed* is of the right column, which represents the desire to impart.

The second of the seven *sefirot* that govern our world is called *Gevurah* (judgement), and is symbolised by the chariot of Isaac, the son for whom Avraham waited a hundred years. The energy of *Gevurah* is called left column, because it is associated with the desire to receive. On *Rosh HaShana* (New Year) we read the portion of the Law called *Akedat Yitzak,* the binding of Isaac, which relates how the left column (Isaac) was tempered or bound by the right column (Avraham), preparing the way for the emergence of the chariot of Jacob. Jacob represents the central column, the essential balancing factor that enables the right column to use the energy of the left without destroying it entirely. *Gevurah* represents judgement, not in the sense of punishment that we usually understand but in the sense of the inevitable repercussions of the exercise of the desire to receive without first removing the aspect of Bread of Shame. Thus we read that "Isaac loved Esau because he did eat of his venison"[68] Esau represents the desire to receive for the body alone, without any desire to impart. Isaac is the means by which that selfish desire transformed into a desire to receive for the sake of imparting by means of the binding of its harmful elements.

Jacob, as we have mentioned, represents the central column which is the *sefira* of *Tiferet* (beauty), as is indicated by the verse, "And Esau was a cunning hunter, a man of the fields, but Jacob was a quiet man, dwelling in tents."[69] The word for 'quiet' in the Torah also has the meaning of 'complete' indicating that with Jacob the system of left, right and central columns was completed. The existence of the central column is the aspect that sets the children of Israel apart from all other races and peoples. It is therefore fitting that Jacob, who is also called Israel,[70] should be the father of the twelve tribes of Israel. These twelve sons, in turn, represent the twelve signs of the zodiac which influence our world; a further example of the completeness that we associate with Jacob. It is also interesting to note, although outside the scope of this book, that the twelve tribes and the twelve signs of the Zodiac are in turn divided into four groups of three, each group being associated with either left, right or central columns.

The fourth chariot is Moses, who represents the *sefira* of *Netzah* (victory), the energy of the right column. The deeper significance of this association will be investigated in a forthcoming book on the significance and meaning of the Festivals, with particular reference to *Pesach (Passover)*. For the present it is sufficient to recall the battle between the Jews and Amalek, on which occasion Moses stood on a hill and controlled the swing of victory by raising or lowering his hands.[71]

It is now possible to return to the question stated early in this book (Chapter II, p.) of why Rabbi Shimon was chosen to write the Zohar, and to the relationship between Moses, Rabbi Akiva and Rabbi Shimon.

Our sages of blessed memory [72] relate the following; "The entire treasure was seen with his eye. This refers to Rabbi Akiva, for that which was not revealed to Moses was revealed to him." Nonetheless, the Talmud states[73] that Moses, through strenuous effort, eventually achieved total comprehension and understanding. A further affinity between Moses and Rabbi Akiva is indicated by our sages as follows: "There were three men who lived 120 years; Moses, Rabbi Yohanan ben Zakkai and Rabbi Akiva." [74] Moses spent forty years in the house of Pharoah, forty years in Midian, and forty years as the shepherd of Israel. Rabbi Akiva's first forty years were spent as an illiterate, his next forty as a student, and his last forty as a teacher. An even more dramatic connection is Moses' plea to the Creator that the understanding of the Torah be transmitted through Rabbi Akiva. [75]

Now it is clear that the soul of Rabbi Akiva, like the souls of all Jews past and present, was present at Mount Sinai when G-d revealed the holy Torah to Moses;[76] why then was it to Moses that the honour of receiving the Word of G-d was given and not to any of the other noble Jewish souls present?

Moses, as we stated, encompassed both the Inner and Encircling Lights. Their power, however, was not sufficient for him to withstand the immense infusion of light that would be transmitted from Mount Sinai. To understand this requires consideration of the spiritual character of the archetypes of Judaism.

The Zohar states that while both Cain and Abel had aspects of the right column it was the weaker of the two in Cain, who was dominated by the left column, whereas Abel had subjected his left column to the rule of the right column.[77] Now the soul of Able was reincarnated within Moses where its good aspects were made manifest.[78] This is the meaning of the verse 'and she saw he was good.'[79] Consequently, Moses was deemed fit to act as a chariot for the supernal wisdom that the Creator imparted to Israel.

On the other hand, while it is obvious that Rabbi Akiva also acquired the necessary degree of spiritual consciousness, the Kabbalah tells us that the root of his soul stemmed from that of Cain.[80] This was to enable him during his lifetime to correct the predominance of the left column, so that his inner spiritual capacity could eventually strike a balance with his evil inclination. For this reason he spent the first forty years of his life, as we have said, as an illiterate, despising the scholars and learned sages of his day[81] and building up the power of his left column. So great was his spiritual potential, which he realised in the last forty years of his life, that he had to enlarge the capacity of his evil inclination as spiritual anchor to his physical world.

Rabbi Shimon, as a reincarnation of Moses, as we stated earlier, and also being possessed of both the Inner and Encircling Lights was chosen to be the transmitter of the Zohar as Moses transmitted the Torah.

The *sefira* of *Hod* (glory) is represented by Aaron, who belonged to the tribe of Levites. The energy here is of the left column, *Hod* being the manifestation of the total energy of the left column in this world.[82] This is indicated by the splendour finery of Aaron's robes when he became *Cohen Gadol* (High Priest) (although it should be noted that the tribe of *Cohen* belongs to the right column).

Joseph, the son of Jacob, is also a chariot of the central column, representing the *sefira* of *Yesod* (foundation). It is through him that all the energy of the upper *sefirot* is brought down onto this physical level. He is the storekeeper who dispenses nourishment to the people, just as he was chosen by the Pharoah to control the sorting and distributing of food in the years of plenty and famine in Egypt.[83]

The last *sefira* is *Malkhut* (kingdom), represented by David. *Malkhut* is the desire to receive, and the world in which we live. Thus we see that David was a man of war and conflict, epitomising the struggle for existence on this physical level. It was because of this warlike nature that he was considered unworthy to build the Temple. More than any other of the Patriarchs, he represented the battle of good and evil that is associated with the 'kingdom' in which we live.[84]

The brief exposition of the nature of the *sefirot* and their connections with the chariots of the Patriarchs should provide the beginner with some new insight into the stories of Torah. On studying them, one should bear in mind at all times the characteristics that we have mentioned here and attempt to understand the events and actions in the light of the aspect of 'bottled-up energy', or *sefira*, that each represents.

Vessels and Lights

The Divine Light of the Creator was not concealed in one action but is gradually transformed by a number of stages; these stages are the vessels appropriate to the quality and quantity of the Light that exists at each level of Tsimtsum.

Vessels are completely the opposite of Lights. The former represent the Desire to Receive, the negative aspect, while the latter express the Desire to Impart, the positive aspect. It is a law of the metaphysical realm that the first vessels to develop after the *Tsimtsum* were those with a greater degree of purity and a consequently lesser degree of the Desire to Receive. The opposite is true of the Lights; here we find that the first Lights to emerge are those with a lesser dgree of the Desire to Impart, and a consequently smaller amount of energy.

The emanation of a complete structure is called *Partzuf,* or countenance. In it will always be found five *Sefirot* or levels of emanation, known as *Keter* (crown), *Hochmah* (wisdom), *Binah* (intelligence), *Tiferet* (beauty), and *Malkhut* (kingdom). The fourth *Sefira,* which is *Tiferet,* contains six *Sefirot: Hesed* (mercy), *Gevurah* (judgment), *Tiferet* (beauty), *Netzah* (victory), *Hod* (majesty) and *Yesod* (foundation).

Keter is the purest vessel, representing the least amount of the Desire to Receive; *Malkhut* represents the epitome and complete manifestation of the Desire to Receive. The various Lights of the soul, commonly referred to as the levels of consciousness, are called *Nefesh* (crude spirit), the lowest level, *Ruah* (spirit), *Neshamah* (soul), *Hayyah* (living) and *Yehidah* (individual), this last being the highest and purest level of the lights. The lights of Nefesh, the lowest level, are first enclothed by the highest vessels, since they are also the first to issue forth from the world of *En Sof.* It should be clear that the upper lights, which appear later, cannot descend to their proper vessels until the lower vessels have unfolded and evolved to permit the lower lights to become enclothed in their respective vessels. This means that until *Nefesh,* the lowest level of spiritual existence, has reached the level of *Malkhut* where it is made manifest in the physical world, none of the higher lights can attain their proper vessels. The paradox we find in this process, whereby the lofty and elevated must wait for the lowly, is a profound expression of the essential duality of the universe; it also explains in greater depth the question touched on earlier, relating to the nature of the levels of spirituality that have existed through the ages, culminating in our age, which is called the Age of the Messiah.

Our generation represents the lowest and final vessel of the *partzuf;* yet it is by virtue of the appearance of this lowly vessel that the lights of *Nefesh* can finally achieve their appointed place. In doing so, a vacuum is created in the upper vessels allowing the upper lights to be drawn down. This is the character of our age, where the gross manifestations of *Nefesh,* the lowest level of spirituality, are revealed in the existence of so many physically-oriented, pleasure-seeking, non-spiritual people, while at the same time we witness the re-awakening of spirituality among the young, and advances in the world of science that threaten to destroy-literally as well as intellectually — all our established concepts of order and purpose.

The question of why the full meaning of the Zohar was not revealed to earlier generations, who were without doubt on a higher level of consciousness and spirituality, and therefore more suited and prepared for it, is no longer a problem. We know that the esoteric mysteries of the Torah and the underlying reasons for the *Mitzvot* are derived from the Lights which are contained in the *Sefirot,* while the practical aspects of ceremonial and ritual grow from the vessels of the *Sefirot* themselves. It follows that earlier generations, whose nature is that of lower levels of soul enclothed in higher levels of vessels, were more complete and developed in the fulfillment of the observances of the practical elements of Torah, whereas our generation will bear witness to the perfect understanding that results from the complete union of the lights with their appointed vessels.

The Middle Point

While many of the main teachings of Kabbalah can be stated in a simple form, it is necessary to remember that some of the concepts of Kabbalistic techniques employ highly intricate explanations and cannot be reduced to simple terms without losing their significance. One such teaching is the concept of the Middle Point, linking in many ways ideas introduced in previous discussions relating to the Creator, Creation and man. More specifically, the concept of the Middle Point sheds light on the difficult problem of Nothingness, both in the spiritual and physical realms. It is particularly relevant to the contemporary issues being raised in the field of physics.

The unfolding, emanation and evolution of 'something from nothing' is frequently described by both the Zohar and the Ari. The symbol used to describe the chain of existence from the 'hidden cause' is the Middle or Primordial Point. This point is what Rabbi Shimon bar Yohai and later Kabbalists refer to as the Beginning: it is the source of all being, the concept which led to all subsequent creations. The first word of the Torah (*Bereshit,* usually translated as 'in the beginning') bears witness to the supreme and paramount importance of the Point of Creation. The abstruse and complex Zoharic interpretation of Creation, in which it describes the emanation of the Middle Point after restriction (*Tsimtsum*) give; a clear indication of the difficulties that will be encountered. It shows here that the entire Torah must be understood on a mystical level if it is to be understood at all. The body of the Torah is no more than a *'corpus symbolicum'* through which the vast fountain of the Divinity and its metaphysical concepts become revealed.

"Know that before the emanations were emanated and the creations were created," declares the Ari, "that the supernal simple light filled the entire existence (within the *En Sof*), and there was no empty space or vacuum whatsoever. For everything was filled with the light of the *En Sof,* the Endless World. However, when the simple desire arose (and restricted itself) to permit creation of the worlds and to emanate emanations and thus bring to fruition the perfection of its deeds, names and appelations, this (restriction) was the cause of the creation of the worlds. And behold the light and its abundance then restricted itself within the middle point.[85]

The Middle Point is so called because it is the vessel for receiving the Endless Light, and is also known as *Sefira* of *Malkhut* (q.v.). However, before restriction the Middle Point (*Malkhut* or Kingdom) was completely and endlessly filled with the upper, supernal Light, beyond any measure or limit. Consequently, this world is designated as the *Olam En Sof*, the Endless World. Here where the Middle Point is united with the Light, encompassed and encircled by it, it is as if the Middle Point were receiving the Light in the exterior of the vessel and is thus filled infinitely and perpetually. In this manner, it is posible for the Middle Point to hold immeasurable and limitless Supreme Light.

From our discussion of the Thought of Creation, we acquainted ourselves with the purpose of the Desire to Receive, which is contained within the endless Light and the Endless World. While this Desire is called the Kingdom *(Malkhut)* of the Endless, nevertheless it did not exert any limitation nor circumscribe any restraint in relation to the Endless Light. At this stage of Creation, the gradations, variations and differentiations of the Desire to Receive were, as yet, unrevealed. Within the Endless World, the Desire to Receive was itself a pure Light and not separated from the Light by any discrimination or severance.

Within this absolute and indivisible unity of the Endless World, there lies a paradox. The supreme Light has the inherent characteristic only of imparting, lacking any degree of the Desire to Receive — yet this Light co-exists with the Desire to Receive which, by its very essence, should bring about a diversity or severance of some sort. At this stage, however, they are considered indiscernible and are in complete and pure unity. The reader might refer to the concept of *Devekuth* for further insight into this problem.

The Infinite Light or Vessel of the *En Sof*, according to Kabbalah, belongs to the area which is totally beyond human comprehension. However, the identity of the Desire to Receive with

—110—

the pure Light can reveal the necessary characteristic of that Desire within the *En Sof* from the standpoint of man. It signifies that the Desire to Receive, despite its innate craving for the Ineffable Goodness, is essentially an embodiment of all other positive characteristics as well — imparting, sharing or bestowing — with an admixture of personal desire and ulterior motives. The mystical interpretation of the Desire to Receive that exists concurrently with the Light within the *En Sof,* is known as the doctrine of the *Sefirot.* This fundamental contemplation of the union between Light and vessel is the common denominator of sharing. — The desire to Impart of the Light and the transmutation of the Desire to Receive — provides us with an indication of the connection between these two opposing forces in the infinite spheres which causes them to be considered inseparable and indiscernible. In this way, we can understand the sublime teaching that the Desire to Receive, did not bring about any boundary or limitation upon the Endless Light, inasmuch as no diversity of essence between them had been revealed at that point.

We are more concerned, however, with the second phase of Creation, leading to an understanding of the relationship between G-d, and His Spiritual Substance of Light that which He created, Creation itself, and the critical part played therein by man, leading to the understanding of our proper objectives in this world.

"Following restriction, whereby the light withdrew around the middle point, there remained an empty space, atmosphere or vacuum surrounding the exact middle point."[86]

This vacuum after restriction should be understood as the first effect. Here lies the entire secret of Kabbalistic thought and I urge the reader to ponder this concept repeatedly. There is no disappearance in light or energy. This we may more fully understand through an example. A fertile male can procreate life almost all of the time. Whether this procreation actually occurs is decided by the vessel or female. If she is sterile then when the seed reaches the vessel (the womb) there is no reaction on the part of the egg. This lack of procreativity we call vacuum. The energy of the male is not diminished. It is the inability of the female to encompass and thus reveal the light or energy. A further example of the mysteries and paradoxes which permeate the teachings of Kabbalah is the concept of 'speed of light'. It is a firm principle in Kabbalistic thought that light is motionless. Therefore the speed of movement can only relate to the vessel, how the vehicle which reveals to us the energy, (light bulb, or lightning), can be measured. The internal energy is immeasurable and timeless. It can be seen as a symbol of profound and penetrating vision which leads to the complete comprehension of the inner meanings and paths of Kabbalah.

Kabbalistic scholars have resorted to figurative terminology in their study of the profound mysteries of Kabbalah, using as referrences the material objects, ideas and functions of our ordinary world. The nature and manner of this symbolic form has been chiefly responsible for the difficulty of penetating into the depths of the inner wisdom of the Kabbalah. Nevertheless, this intricate and at times confusing maze of symbolism is the very key to its understanding. This paradox can be understood if we consider the use of imagery in other forms of writing and common usage, where we often use one concept to illuminate another. Thus, when we refer to prayers and *mitzvot* as 'cables', we are using the image to emphasise the drawing aspect, or their function as paths through which certain sorts of energy can be channelled, just as electricity can be transmitted through a cable. We are not, however, referring to the physical characteristics of a cable, such as its dimensions, shape or colour, and anyone who does not realise this is likely to mistake our original intention. It is the same with the use of images and symbols in the Kabbalah, where one specific attribute of a physical entity may be referred to by using the image of the whole entity. If we are aware of the precise usage we can learn from the symbol, but if we select the wrong attribute, or impute superfluous attributes, we will be misled. It should be borne in mind at all times that all the words of the Kabbalah are but images and symbols, since words alone cannot express the inexpressible mystery of the Creation.

In determining and expressing ideas concerned with the invisible world, the scholars of the Kabbalah have made use of the names of the tangible dimensions of this world. In effect each name symbolises, explains, and represents its own upper entity, which is located in the constellation of the celestial regions. From this we learn that the lower realm is patterned after the upper, preceding realm, as we read in the Zohar: "Nor does the smallest blade of grass on the earth fail to have its specially appointed star in the heavens."[87]

All that exists in the celestial or supernal world will, in time, prevail and show itself in a reflected image on earth, yet the totality of upper and lower worlds are always one whole entity. This provides the insight and knowledge required for our understanding of metaphysical concepts.

The upper and lower worlds can be compared to a tree when we come to consider the picture of Creation, by which the natural laws and principles of both metaphysical and physical realms operate in our universe. It is the tree of energy, with its feedback of activity, the 'Tree of Life' referred to in the Zohar,[88] and the *'Etz Hayim'* of the Ari, in which he devised what has come to be recognised as the most comprehensive and lucid interpretation and systematic description of the Zohar. The tree of life has its roots buried deep underground, beyond the realm of perception; all we see are the results, or effects of that root, in the form of trunk branches, and leaves. Thus through the principles of corresponding natures we can observe the unknown areas of the upper realm by examining the interactions of that which is below. With the knowledge of Kabbalah, we can trace the origin and development of those cosmic forces and principles which ultimately influence the behavioral patterns of man, and shape the course of mundane history.

The source of all reality takes place in the upper, undetected sphere, (the root)descending and evolving through the process of cause and effect (or imparting and receiving) in an intelligible order down to the level of our existence. The physical universe, with its cosmic elements, is the bodying forth or evolution of the spiritual region (trunk, branches, etc.). There is no wisdom or science to be found whose objects and functions are so closely integrated as in the law of cause and effect, which is the infinite progression of the esoteric knowledge of the Kabbalah.

We can now better understand that stage in the evolutionary process of Creation in which, following the restriction of the Middle Point, which is the Desire to Receive, a vacuum or empty space was established.

At this point, declares the Ari, "there were no distinguishable or discernible levels or grades, despite the withdrawal of the light."[89] Why then, we might be justified in asking, are we witnesses to an indisputedly multi-faceted Creation? "The distinction of a multitude of manifestations," answers the Zohar, "is due solely and primarily to our way of perceiving the world, a result of the perception of the light by finite, created beings."[90] Furthermore, from what we have said regarding the relationship between upper and lower worlds, it must follow that the infinite manifestations of our terrestrial realm are a metaphorical indication of the yet more remotely hidden worlds of the celestial regions.

The innermost being of the Divinity, the Light as an extension of the Deity, motivated and initiated the creation of the soul and the *Sefirot* (q.v.), vessels which would ultimately enclothe and benefit from its beneficence. The motivating Thought of Creation, which was to impart beneficence to man, through the Desire to Receive, influenced the emergence of the multiform degrees of the Desire to Receive. This is due to the fundamental characteristic of the Light, which could fill and nourish these vessels with an infinite quantity of abundance. In other words the Light, in its infinite Desire to Impart, necessitated and caused the manifestation of a correspondingly infinite number of souls which would desire this beneficence. Thus this first and primary world, the world of *En Sof* (the Infinite), is given this symbolic name in accordance with the endless variety of degree of receiving that took place within the union of the Light with the Kingdom of the *En Sof*. In all this it should be remembered that the Divine Light itself remained a total unity, as noted in the passage, "I am the Lord, I do not change."[91]

We can compare this process of undiminished imparting to other varieties of power and energy — the endless waterfall, which can fill an infinite number of vessels without being affected, or an electric current that can supply power for a wide range of appliances which may differ in their subsequent manifestation of that power (light, heat, motion) without affecting the source of the energy. In all these cases, the division which is ultimately seen is a result and dependent on the energy of the source, which is enclothed and confined within the vessels. In the source of the energy itself, however, there is no change.

Let us now return to the section of the Zohar that deals with the opening lines of the story of Creation, bearing in mind that the 'beginning' referred to is the emergence of the Middle Point.

"When the desire of the king began to take effect," declares the Zohar, "a hard spark (as from the striking of two stones, one 'rejecting' the other and thus producing a spark, as with the Desire to Receive in its rejection of the flow of light from the Desire to Impart) engraved engravings in the Upper Supernal Light (thus causing a vacuum, just as in the hewing of a stone, which at the moment of the chisel's stroke, leaves an empty space in the stone and causes a spark, which is otherwise known as the spark of friction). This hard spark sprang forth within the innermost recesses of the mystery of the *Olam En Sof*, the Endless, (the final phase of the Endless, which is referred to as *Malkhut* of the Endless World) as a potential and formless concept of aura, indiscernible and undected, wedged into a ring. This is the mystery of the Middle Point which, before the Restriction, was unutterable and inexpressible, but at this stage, is expressible to the extent of being comparable to a circle in that it has not beginning or end nor phases by which it can be detected, so that it is indiscernible. It is neither white nor black, neither red nor green."[92]

The Zohar, in stressing that it was "not black", seeks to avoid the misunderstanding that might arise when considering the restriction of the Light. Since it is discussing the withdrawal of the Light, it might seem that the state of 'absence of Light' was the same as blackness, this being its customary definition. However, in its determination to render the exact nature of the stage which became manifested immediately outside the Endless world, emerging as the act of restriction, the Zohar insists that this particular stage, being totally imperceptible, lacks any of the attributes of colour — including the total lack of it.

After the *Tsimtsum*, or restriction, whereby the vessel of *Malkhut* (Desire to Receive) brought about a separation from and rejection of the Endless Light, the desire of the vessel was in no way diminished. We can see this from the story which appears further on in this book of the rich man and the poor man (page 133); when the poor man refuses the food (restriction), he does not thereby affect his hunger in any way — he merely states that he is unable to exercise his Desire to Receive under the circumstances, due to his feeling of Bread of Shame. Here too the desire for spiritual nourishment remains constant.

Since the inherent nature of the Light is to impart, it continues to attempt to fulfill the desires of the vessel, as it did continuously in the *Olam En Sof*. However, at the moment of restriction when the vessel brought about the separation, the Light withdrew. The Zohar talks of the return of the "Line of Light" from the *En Sof* because its return in its entire form would have led to the re-awakening of the feeling of Bread of Shame, since the vessel had not, at this stage, been able to do anything to share that which it wanted to receive.

The return of a circumscribed and limited measure of Light obviously failed to fill the vessel completely, as we have said. This paved the way for the vessel to overcome the Bread of

Shame, which is the fundamental purpose for the creation of the worlds, culminating in the creation of our universe. Due to its insatiable desire for the limitless Goodness of the *En Sof,* which remained unfulfilled by the limited return of the line of Light, the Desire to Receive now became recognisable through its exertions to satisfy its desire. Prior to the Restriction, when all desires were instantly fulfilled, the Desire to Receive was motionless and indiscernable due to its union with the Light (*Devekuth*). It is only after the separation, after the vacuum and the return of the line of Light, that an awareness of something lacking comes into being within the vessel. At that point, movement comes into being, indicating the emanation of the world of time, space and motion in which we exist, prior to our removal of that aspect of Bread of Shame and our subsequent re-unification with the Blessed world of the *En Sof.*

R. Abba was once going from Cappadocia to Lydda in company with R. Jose. As they were going they saw a man approaching with a mark on his face. R. Abba called to him and said: 'Tell me, what is that mark on your face?' He replied: 'I was once travelling with my sister, and we turned in to an inn, where I drank much wine. All that night I was in company with my sister. In the morning I found the host quarrelling with another man. I interposed between them and received blows from both and was severely wounded, but was saved by a doctor'. R. Abba asked who the doctor was, and he replied: 'It was R. Simlai'. 'What medicine did he give you?' asked R. Abba. He replied: 'Spiritual healing.

Zohar III, P. 75b.

PART THREE

MAKING THE CONNECTION
PRACTICAL APPLICATIONS

Everyday below is controlled by a day above. Now an act below stimulates a corresponding activity above. Thus if a man does kindness on earth, he awakens loving kindness above, and it rests upon that day which is crowned therewith through him. Similarly if he performs a deed of mercy, he crowns that day with mercy and it becomes his protector in the hour of need.

Zohar III, P. 92a.

CHAPTER X

OPERATIONAL TOOLS

Although the Kabbalah deals with matters of an elevated spiritual nature, it does so with the sole intention of providing the Jew with tools of a high enough quality for him to fulfill his own potential. The teachings of Kabbalah are not intended to be confined to the realms of abstact thought processes or disciplines learned for the sake of discipline alone, but should lead directly to the application of those elevated thoughts and methods of learning in the realm of action. Moreover, the intellectual substance of the Torah is of a special and unique nature providing the Jewish people with tools for the soul which, properly understood, will enable them to articulate in the world of action what is asked of them in the world of thought and feeling.

A Kabbalistic analysis of the mitzvot, the commandments of Torah, gives the practicing Jew an immediate insight into essence of all manifestations on the physical level, by demonstrating how the eternal laws of the universe manifest themselves in the context of our material world. Those people who regard the precepts as outmoded or irrelevant are ignorant of their true nature, which is that of conduits or cables through which Divine revelation, omnipotent beneficence, the profound wisdom of the Creator, and the metaphysical laws and principles of the universe are revealed and understood.

The Zohar, sensing that the mitzvot are but profound symbols filled with priceless and unguessed treasures, goes far beyond the customary approaches to knowledge, as we shall see.

Rabbinic authorities have classified many of the *mitzvot* as *Hukim,* or statutes, meaning laws that are ordained by Torah, and which we are to observe even though a reasonable or meaningful explanation cannot be given. Some commentators have seen these statutes as an example of the absolute compliance to the decrees of the Creator that is required of the Jewish people as an indication of their faith. The Kabbalah, however, reveals the broader arena of doctrine and statute that flows from our Torah, where strict observance is combined with a fundamental belief in the legitimacy and necessity of inquiry. In explaining the significance and function of each mitzvah, philosophical discourses that do not have a basis in the sublime and eternal wisdom of the Kabbalah are bound to lead to divergent, or even opposing points of view, whereas the root knowledge contained in Kabbalah reveals the eternal nature of the unchanging truth that is contained in every word of Torah. The Kabbalistic attitude towards the fulfillment of these precepts no longer reflects a dogmatic approach whereby the individual is required to demonstrate his allegiance to the Lord by adhering rigorously to the confines of strict obedience. There are many areas, the Kabbalah tells us, where our feeble mental capacity is totally unable to grasp the understanding of the mysteries of the universe and of its Creator, but within these limitations there are also many aspects of our world that are revealed through knowledge of the workings of the metaphysical realm.

True religion is a path along which the seeker no longer gropes in blindness and fear; it is a path that has been trodden in the full light of wisdom by the sages of the past, who have forseen the problems and pitfalls that would face the novice, and have shared with us their knowledge so that their example should be a light for future generations. True religion deals with the firm principles and laws of the universe, cognisant of the fact that any deviation from that path might result in physical as well as emotional disturbances. It can be regarded as the system of laws which governs and generates the physical and ethical laws of the world we live in. The religious man thus becomes one who has knowledge of the workings of this higher system and of its applications and implications in the lower physical world.

The Kabbalistic philosophy regarding Divine commandments and ritual is best described by the legend of Hillel. According to this legend, a recent convert to Judaism came before Hillel and asked him if it was possible to teach the entire Torah while standing on one leg; Hillel replied, "That which is hateful to you, do not do unto your neighbour. This is the entire Torah. The remaining decrees and commandments are but a commentary on this basic principle."[93]

This exchange raises a great number of intriguing problems. What, firstly, was the intention of the convert in asking his question? Was he expressing cynical doubt about his new-found religion, seeking a 'short cut' to Judaism through the wisdom of the Rabbi, or was he sincere in his search for the touchstone of Jewish thought and practice? Then we might ask whether Hillel's reply is merely intended to silence a foolish student, or whether it truly contains the essence of Torah. The difficulty connected with Hillel's answer lies in the fact that the mitzvot are divided into two categories: those directed at the relationship between Israel and the Creator, and those concerned with Israel and his fellow man. How, then, can the one precept of "love your neighbour as yourself" include all the precepts of the Torah, as Hillel seems to be saying, including even those relating to man and his maker? Furthermore with regard to the latter part of his reply are we to understand that all six hundred and twelve precepts merely explain the one basic ethical law and precept of "love your neighbour".

A close examination of the dialogue reveals the very essence and purpose of the Torah. The convert's request refers to the ultimate objectives of Torah — the termination of the path along which deeds and service lead. The entire content of the Torah, its laws and commandments, are nothing more than instruments for the improvement and development of self-control. Therefore Hillel chose the one precept of "love your neighbour" as the one specific idea that can guide men to this final goal. The precept reveals the inner spirituality of the individual, the incarnation of the truly Divine within him, and thus draws him closer to the source of Light and beauty. This source, which we have called the Desire to Impart, is the chief characteristic by which we can come to know the Creator.

We learn from the Book of Genesis that "the inclination of man's heart is evil from his youth."[94] This refers to the essence of man, the Desire to Receive which, until the age of religious majority dominates all actions in the guise of a Desire to Receive for oneself alone. The actions of a child are motivated by this essence, without any regard for others and without any Desire to Impart to anyone else.

Upon reaching the age of (*bar* or *bat Mitzvah*) — thirteen years for a boy, twelve for a girl — the individual is incarnated with a *Yetzer Ha'tov*, a good inclination, which is a potential metaphysical form of energy similar to the Creator's Desire to impart. From that age onwards, the concept of "Love your neighbour" becomes the link connecting all that exists in the celestial heights with the lower level of this world. Man is the channel through which the Creator's beneficience and grace flow from the upper heavenly spheres to the corporeal world. The degree and intensity of this union, however, depends on the extent to which human egocentricity transforms itself into the Desire to Impart, since the nature of a channel or cable is to transmit energy, not to absorb it. We can compare this to the result of placing a curtain in front of the light of the sun; the thicker the curtain, representing the Desire to Receive the more light it will absorb into itself, while a thin curtain will present less obstruction to the passage of the light. It should be clear from this example that the thinner curtain has a greater affinity with the original source of light — the sun. Although it has no light of its own, it nonetheless has the aspect of the Desire to Impart, which is the essential quality of light, in that it does not hinder the passage of the light. The thick curtain, on the other hand, through its absorption of light, takes on the opposite characteristic, the Desire to Receive, thus bringing about a separation of function between it and the sun.

If this identity of function is the final destination of the soul, the intimate and permanent union that results from the conformity of Divine and human wills, then we must direct our attention to the words of our Talmudic sages concerning the Evil inclination: "The Creator, in addressing Himself to the human will, declares, 'I created an evil inclination, and also the Torah with its commandments and rituals as a means for the transformation of the evil inclination.'" Torah study and observance of its precepts gradually nurture the individual until he is sufficiently disciplined to remove all traces of this "love for oneself only", so that all his deeds are sanctified by a desire to impart to others. The ethical and moral commandments that apply between man and his neighbour secure for the individual the structure of the aspect of selflessness which is implied by the concept of "love your neighbour".

We can therefore understand the words of Hillel to the convert more profoundly: by achieving the goal of loving our neighbour, we are transforming our inherent Desire to Receive for ourselves only, which separates us from the Creator, into the Desire to Impart which, through its identity of form with the Creator's imparting aspect, draws us closer to Him and thus fulfills the original thought of Creation.

A more specific analysis of the rituals relating to man and his Creator, an area all too often neglected in rabbinic teaching, will reveal a fundamental and extraordinary expression of moral religious consciousness. To place obedience at the pinnacle of the aims of the Mitzvot and to interpret ritual and ceremonial observance of Torah as a revelation of dogmatic precepts leading to unquestioning subservience is to to deny the spiritual origin of Divine commandments. It suffices merely to compare strict religious observance in the course of the last two hundred years with present adherence to Biblical law to realise the result of such an approach. Judaism is no longer spiritual and experiential but has developed into a rigid moral code, repellent to all but a small minority of the faithful. The teachings of Kabbalah, in all their many forms, have yet to succeed in establishing once again the bridge linking the fundamental instincts of the individual Jew faced with the demands and strains of daily life with the quest for the inner meaning of the transcendent element of the celestial world.

The rituals and precepts that concern themselves with the relationship between man and his maker would seem to have lost, in our times, their distinctive spirituality. The wisdom of the Kabbalah reveals them again in their orginal light, however, enabling us to see them not merely as a test of our obedience and faith, but as an active conditioning agent as powerful and vital to spiritual progress as any of the precepts relating to moral and ethical law. One of the most clear examples of the interweaving of ritual and moral instruction is the law concerning *Tefillin* (phylacteries), which applies to all males who have reached the age of thirteen. A true understanding of this precept, which is given to us in the Kabbalah, enables us to see it as a tool by which we can further our journey towards the goal of "love your neighbour", and not as the commemorative or submissive act for which it is all too often mistaken.

One of the most important chapters in the early part of the Bible is that concerning the binding of Isaac — the *Akedah,* as it is known in Hebrew.[95] The story itself is too well known to need repeating here, it being sufficient to recall the problems that it raises.

Abraham has prayed for an heir, and at the advanced age of one hundred his request had been granted. It is this son, Isaac, that he is now asked to offer up as a sacrifice to G-d. This seems incomprehensible on a superficial level of understanding: was Abraham's willingness to slaughter his own son a necessary or justified test of his complete surrender to the service of the Almighty? The Torah would seem to suggest that the supreme test applied solely to Abraham, as it states, "G-d tested Abraham",[96] yet the strain placed on Isaac's allegiance would seem to be as great, if not greater. Isaac is at this time thirty-seven years old, yet the Torah seems to ignore completely his absolute submission to the Will of the Creator, emphasising Abraham's selflessness.

"The text," observes the Zohar, "requires explanation". We should have expected the verse to read, 'G-d tested Isaac', and not Abraham — after all, Isaac was already thirty-seven years old, and no longer under his father's jurisdiction'; he could have easily refused, without rendering his father liable to punishment. Why, therefore, does it say 'G-d tested Abraham' instead of 'G-d tested Isaac'? The truth, however, is that it (the testing of Abraham) was required. In order for Abraham to attain perfection, he had to be invested with the attribute of the left (negative) column of Isaac, of which Abraham was not characteristic. Abraham is symbolic of the right (positive) column, which is called *Hesed* (mercy). But perfection does not exist unless there is a balance of both positive and negative. This we can observe even on our mundane level, where a total unit consists of a harmonious relationship between positive and negative. In this story, water (mercy, or right column, represented by Abraham) would be united with fire (vigour, or left column, represented by Isaac), through which it would be possible for Abraham to administer justice and make it a part of his character. For whoever saw a father's heart turn from compassion to cruelty?" asks the Zohar. However, the object here was to temper the discord between fire and water so that they should be settled in their places until Jacob (central column, the agent of synthesis) appeared. Only then would all be in order and the triad of the patriarchs (the complete system of connections and balance) be completed. It is thus instructive to note that the word *'nisa'*, usually translated as 'tested', also means 'lifted up' or 'elevated' — meaning, in this context, 'brought together at a higher level'. The celestial level was firmly established on the terrestrial level as a result of Abraham's actions, so that a synthesis could occur."[97]

From the interpretation of the Zohar, it would seem that the demand for Abraham's unconditional surrender was not the intent of the Creator. The 'binding of Isaac', which represents the focal point of the episode, involves the bringing together of two forces, providing the Jew with a system by which he can develop and achieve harmony within himself and can subsequently connect with the source of Light, the Creator.

Abraham, symbolising the right or imparting column, could not achieve wholeness unless he became one with the left or receiving column. This does not mean that he had to negate or destroy the left column, as is indicated by the verse, "And Abraham stretched forth his hand, and took the knife to slay his son, whereupon the Angel of the Lord called unto him and said, 'Lay not your hand upon the lad''.[98] The binding of the left (Isaac) by the right (Abraham) is the procedure through which man achieves perfection by way of his central column (Jacob), his thinking or mental capacity, symbolised by the centrally-located head.

This, then, was the occasion of the bringing together of these two opposing energy forces, the vehicle through which the metaphysical energy of the binding of the left column was connected for all time to the physical level. It is this same harmonising influence that we connect with when we bind *Tefillin* on the left arm — a ritual observance which, when understood in the light of the Kabbalah, can be seen in its true, profound and moralistic meaning.

The revelation of the significance of *Tefillin* serves as a model for understanding how the Kabbalah comprehends and interprets the *mitzvot*. Another example is provided by the question of *Kashrut,* the dietary laws relating to the separation of milk from meat.[99] All too often this *Mitzvah* is regarded as an indication of complete submission to the Divine Will, or even as an outward and visible sign of the Jewishness of a household. The Kabbalah, however, approaches the subject from an altogether different viewpoint.[100] It distinguishes between meat, which is red in colour, and milk, which is white. Is this merely a chance occurrence, or can we assume that an ordered universe will be reflected at all levels of existence? Thus, says the Kabbalah, red represents the left column, whose attribute is *Din* (judgement) and whose function is to receive. The meat of an animal is a result or product of everything that the animal takes into itself, exemplifying the Desire to Receive. Milk, on the other hand, represents the right column, the Desire to Share, and the aspect of *Hesed* (mercy, giving); its colour — white — includes all other colours, thereby indicating that it represents in its essential characteristic of giving and nourishment the highest level to which man can aspire. It is clear that the two elements represented by meat and milk are in opposition to one another — one is *Din* (judgement), the other *Hesed* (mercy). The outpouring of milk signifies life for the offspring, whereas the shedding of blood signifies death and separation from life. We have seen in the example of Abraham and Isaac, how fundamentally opposed elements can be brought together; here, we see two mutually exclusive elements that we are instructed to separate from one another. The Zohar goes on to give the reasons for this difference, too, but such distinctions are beyond the scope of this introductory book.

A similar example of the necessity for the separation of blood (in its aspect of *din*) from life is found in the laws relating to the menstrual cycle (*niddah*), which obligate every Jewish couple to observe a period of separation.[101] During the period of *niddah,* a woman's body is subject to the power of Judgement, signified by the appearance of blood and by other changes in her psychological make-up. Therefore she cannot come into contact with the life-giving forces of the marriage union, represented by the white colour of the sperm. There is a clear and grave warning here that death and life must be respected in this world for what they represent — two separate and irreconcilable elements.[102]

It is thus obvious that in each of the six hundred and thirteen mitzvot there is an underlying reason — not just an outward sign of devotion, but an instruction regarding the usefulness or danger of some aspect of the universe. Whereas the Torah and Talmud give us a general idéa of the nature of these aspects, only the Kabbalah reveals their true identity as tools with which we can work to achieve the goal of unity with the Creator. The mitzvot exist in order to enable us to keep a balance in the universal forces of energy that resulted from the Creation.[103] The ultimate balance, we learn from Hillel, and the ultimate *mitzvah* is the relationship between a man and his fellow, guided at all times by the principle of 'love your neighbour as yourself'. The rest, indeed, is commentary.

Chapter XI

DEVEKUTH — THE CIRCULAR CONCEPT

The union of upper and lower, the bringing together of opposites which was touched on in the previous chapter, brings us full circle in the chain of metaphysical events by which the universe is structured. In relation to the union of man with his Creator, this concept is known as *Devekuth,* or cleaving.

Union with G-d is fundamentally a bringing together of metaphysical entities. Just as the separation or union of tangible objects is accomplished by either removing them from each other or by bringing one part closer to the other in space, so it is with metaphysical or spiritual forces. Separation or union is achieved through the transformation of contrasting phases which either sever or unite.

The Creator is, as we have said, purely a bestower; He imparts without being in any way diminished by imparting and receives nothing in return. In this, He is the measure of the perfect donor. Mankind, on the contrary, has a perpetual and unfulfilled craving for the fulfillment of its needs and desires, due to its eternal Desire to Receive; this is the vital intention within the Thought of Creation. The Desire to Receive is thus both a mark of man's essence and also the cause of the separation of his being from that of the Crator. This chasm is widened when man preceives himself as being a receptacle for his own benefit alone, when his vessel attempts to capture and contain the Light with no thought of sharing or imparting it to others. Thus, while his natural instinct is towards self-reliance rather than reliance on others, he is still aware through the influence of his consciousness that he is very much reliant on the bounty of the Creator. This awareness, however, ultimately leads to the inevitable conclusion that receiving G-d's beneficence is only for the purpose of rendering delight to the Creator.

The two alternatives — receiving purely for oneself or accepting G-d's beneficence in order to share with others and thus rendering Him great delight — are mutually exclusive. It would appear that we are caught in a trap, for by putting ourselves at the mercy of the Creator's bounty, we experience Bread of Shame because we have received something for nothing and rely on that which we have not earned. This, the Zohar teaches, is the complete opposite of what in fact happens. By accepting the Creator's beneficence, we are fulfilling not only the role of our own individual creation, but also of the original Thought of Creation. This can only happen, however, if we are aware of the correct way in which to give and to receive. This, as we have said, is the purpose of Kabbalah, which literally means Receiving. In the balanced relationship between donor and recipient, the aspect of Bread of Shame is rendered void, since we have created a situation in which, although there is giving and taking, it is equal measure on both sides, so that there is no feeling of lack or shame.

We find this idea elaborated in a treatise of the Talmud regarding the laws of the marriage ceremony.[104] It is specified that during the ceremony the man is required to present a wedding ring to his bride, by which exchange she becomes his legal wife. This is the Mosaic law, and the reasons supporting it will be considered more fully in a volume on the concept of soulmates, marriage and divorce. The Talmud, however, cites one occasion where the traditional order of the marriage ceremony is reversed. When the bridegroom is a man of great merit, due to his devotion to the study of Torah, the bride may give the wedding ring to him, instead of he to her, and on his reciting the traditional formula, 'you shall by this become betrothed to me', she then becomes his legal wife. The Talmud explains that 'through his recipiency, the marriage has become legalised by her delight in receiving the pleasure in being honoured by virtue of his acceptance of the ring, although the legal procedure has been reversed'.[105]

In most marriages the *Halacha* is followed, and the man gives a material token (a ring or coin) as a symbol of marriage.[106] The important point to note here is that the significance of his act is the giving, the token ring or coin being of no intrinsic value. However, in the exceptional case we have described, we are forced to conclude that the bridegroom's act of receiving the ring from his bride is in itself regarded as an act of giving. Instead of giving her a coin or ring, which is a material symbol, he presents her with the far more lofty and spiritual delight of honouring her by marriage. Receiving that is undertaken for the sole purpose of imparting constitutes absolute, complete bestowal. Thus the groom in this instance is considered by the sages of the Talmud to be giving more by receiving the ring than he would if he were to give it. In the case of the Godly man his very marriage is an act of giving, so that the ring, the symbol of consummation, is passed from woman to man. There is also an equivalent heightening in the transference of spiritual energy, since by her act of giving, the bride is receiving and, more to the point, she is receiving far more than she would have done had she merely received the ring from the man. In this heightened dynamic interchange of energy, the relationship is consummated, and the Bread of Shame is totally banished. Indeed, one might argue that the reversal of the normal marriage procedure when the groom is especially learned, since if this were not the case, the bride would be only receiving and would therefore be susceptible to the Bread of Shame. However, when she gives the ring to the man, she elevates her role of recipient to that of donor, and brings the necessary balance to the relationship.

There is a tale told by Kabbalists which illustrates this initially confusing concept clearly. The tale concerns a certain wealthy man who invited a number of friends to join him on some festive occasion. Just as the company was about to sit down to the festive meal, the host noticed a poor man passing by. He felt sorry for the man and instructed one of the servants to invite him in. All the guests could see that the poor man was badly in need of food and clothing, yet when the host cordially invited him to join them and share the meal, they were astonished to hear him refuse. The host, bewildered and mystified by the unexpected reply, urged the poor man to reconsider, only to be told that he (the poor man) had no need for this sort of charity. The host insisted, the poor man politely refused, and so the conversation continued until the poor man finally threw his hands in the air in a gesture of helplessness and said, "Very well, if it really means that much to you, I'll accept your kind hospitality." With a sigh of relief, the company sat down to begin the festivities.

In this story, as in the example of the special marriage, the roles of donor and recipient are reversed, resulting in a heightening and sanctification of the transaction. To the receiver — the poor man — the request that he receive beneficence without due regard to his having earned this kindness appears initially as something degrading: this is identical to the concept of Bread of Shame. Thus what appeared to be simple generosity on the part of the host takes on a new aspect in the light of the poor man's inability to share or impart anything and so remove the Bread of Shame. It emerges as something unwanted — not bcause the poor man is not in need of food, but because there is no way in which he can take it as yet without losing his self-respect. Faced with the choice between humiliation and hunger, it is perhaps no longer surprising that he refuses the food. A receiver who is not prepared to share or who is prevented from sharing will inevitably reject the true intention of the donor. This built-in metaphysical rejection became inevitable after the initial feeling of Bread of Shame was experienced by the souls in the world of *En Sof.*

However, once this unexpected refusal of an obviously desired gift has taken place the flow of energy in the situation begins to change. The rich man realises that he has been deprived of an opportunity to do good, and begins to become more insistent and pleading. In effect, he is now no longer offering the poor man food but asking him a favour — that he afford him the opportunity of sharing some of his wealth, and of receiving pleasure from that sharing. The poor man now experiences a situation where he is being asked to impart as well as receive and therefore consents to join the feast. The rich man, too, is both giving and receiving. The cycle has been completed, with flow and feedback now in a state of dynamic balance.

We can apply this example to any form of benevolence: unless there is this balance between donor and receiver, the original intention of the donor will not be realised. This holds true on all levels, from the original Thought of Creation which was to impart Ineffable Goodness to man, and which will only be realised finally when we have learnt properly how to receive, and interact on the level of family, friendships and business.

The foregoing analysis reveals the fundamental necessity for this 'circular concept'. It is bound up not only with the redemption of the individual soul, but also with the redemption of all souls that is associated with the age of the Messiah. Through the circular concept, it becomes possible to convert the Desire to Receive into a Desire to Impart, transmuting, we might say, the letter M in "me" to the letter W in "we": the first points downwards, emphasising the connection with the physical world, while the second reaches up towards the Heavens, indicating its affinity with the concept of *Devekuth,* or communion with G-d. Through this affinity of desires, we are brought closer to the structure of the Creator's Desire to Impart and can free ourselves from the stigma of being able only to receive for ourselves. From our earthly existence we are led to a higher spiritual level of consciousness, to a liberation from the tyranny of the five senses, and to a higher realm of spiritual existence.

Devekuth, in kabbalistic terms, is a profound concept but by no means unattainable. Love of man — or for that matter, love of G-d — are not merely mystical or theological concepts, but rather a path of life through which the realm of metaphysics can be permanently united with earthly reality, thus liberating the true spiritual nature of man. It is not a teaching of austerity of asceticism, against which the sages often warned. One is not required to relinquish all the material possessions and physical comforts that are associated with corporeal existence in order to achieve spiritual growth. Indeed, Devekuth is realised within the framework of the physical world more effectively through social intercourse and commitment to society than by seclusion and self-denial, as Hillel implied in his answer to the convert (q.v.). *Mitzvot,* as we have seen, can be divided into two categories: those concerned with the relationship between Israel and Creator, and those that govern the relationship between Israel and his fellow man. In working towards the ultimate objective of *Devekuth,* the gradual transformation of receiving for oneself into receiving in order to share, those precepts between man and man are more likely to lead the individual to the goal by reason of their ever-changing role and position in the daily demands of existence. The differentiation of desires that we find in our dealings with those around us forces us to explore in real terms the meaning of 'love your neighbour', and to recognise the diversity that has existed since the En Sof. Through this diversity we shall eventually remove the aspect of Bread of Shame and return to the Blessed Endless.

In the process of spiritual elevation, each person is obliged to express his innermost potential of giving (and therefore, as we have understood, of receiving also), so as to achieve his own elevation, which permits the ultimate measure of beneficence and fulfillment from the Creator. Stated in simple terms, the precepts that regulate the interactions of men are the ideal conditioning agents for transforming man's basic character. These precepts are designed specifically to re-align the selfish aspect of desire with the intention of the Creator, Whose fundamental characteristic is that of imparting.

This, then, is the core of Hillel's reply. 'Love your neighbour' is, quite simply, the principal and most effective means of attaining *Devekuth,* which is the goal and purpose of Torah. The unifying force of this love, through which the individual may discover and draw on the innermost potential of his own positive qualities, assures the continuing progress of human development, inasmuch as the Desire to Receive has been kept in check.

The literal meaning of the word *Devekuth* reveals the very essence of man's relationship with G-d and with his fellow man. It implies attachment, a cleaving of two while appearing to be a complete unit, nevertheless retain their individual characteristics. The Torah uses the same root to describe the relationship between a man and a woman, a union which is considered as making both parties whole, in that each brings what is lacking from the other to the relationship. The word *'davok',* meaning 'to attach' is used to describe this union, as it is to portray man's union with G-d.

Thus we find in the concept of *Devekuth* a central virtue by which each individual, and thus mankind as a whole, can reach his objective in this world, the goal of transmuting the elemental characteristic of man into the fundamental characteristic of the Creator. The core of man, as represented by his actions, is bound up with the essence of the Creator, leading to the elimination of the Bread of Shame and thus fulfilling the initial purpose of the Creation. If the essence of the *Mitzvot* is their conditioning ability, providing man with the tools with which to attain his objective, it follows that knowledge and understanding of these precepts are linked closely to their observance.

This aspect of knowledge in its relation to observance and ultimately to *Devekuth* is revealed in the passage from the Torah in which Solomon is advised, "Know the G-d of thy father, and serve him with an entire heart and a willing soul."[107] What is the nature of this 'knowledge' of G-d? Have we not been saying throughout this book that the Creator is beyond the scope of understanding and knowledge? A closer analysis of the concept of *Devekuth* will enable us to understand the true meaning and application of this injunction.

"And Adam knew Eve his wife; and she conceived and bore Cain."[108] In this sentence we find a revelation of *Devekuth,* the union of man and woman expressed by the verb meaning to know or understand, succeeded by an attachment. The knowledge of G-d, is essentially a mental process similar to this physical one — an understanding of His fundamental characteristics, which is followed by clinging or *'cleaving'* to the Divine Will. The aspect of understanding is related to the transformation of the Desire to Receive into the Desire to impart, this being the essential nature of the creator. All we can know about Him is that he is good, and His desire is to share. When we have fully understood this, not just with the intellect but with our entire being, it will follow that we will seek to emulate Him in that essential quality, and thus, as we have described, draw closer to Him through an increasing similarity of our nature to His.

While we have repeatedly stressed the unity of Torah and all its commandments, we seem to be making a distinction here between two sets of *mitzvot.* In fact, it should be clear that there is no distinction to be drawn between the goals of these two aspects of *mitzvot* — rather, any apparent difference is a reflection of the current state of Judaism. There are many Jews who, while less than Orthodox, would nevertheless still claim to uphold the moral and social laws of the Torah — those between man and man. It is the laws concerning ritual, which are seen as a relic of the past, that are rejected. The Orthodox establishment, on the other hand, has sometimes gone to opposite extremes. Having what amounts to a monopoly over the ritual laws that cover the relationship between man and his Creator, they have often abandoned or neglected the moral laws concerning our obligations to our neighbours. Needless to say both tendencies are regrettable, since they indicate a lack of understanding of the true purpose of the whole Torah. The current state of Judaism is therefore yet another reason for the importance of the revelation for Kabbalah today.

Those *mitzvot* between man and his Creator constitute, for a large number of Jews, the central tradition, ceremonial and ritual of Judaism. For these religious concepts, untold numbers of Jews throughout history have fought, suffered and died, placing the freedom to observe these signs of their faith above their own lives. Yet these selfsame *mitzvot* now appear to have caused a dangerous alienation among a large segment, if not the vast majority, of contemporary Jews. Moreover, the barrier between those who adhere to these *mitzvot* and the mass of the people has been constantly hardening.

It would be some consolation if the Orthodox community stressed the spiritual nature of the precepts so that it could be appreciated by the mass of non-observant or non-ritualistic Jews. According to our sages, one who performs his ritual obligations correctly will also be a model of supreme moral sensitivity and social awareness.[109] This, regretfully, is not the case at present, since we have witnessed an often alarming separation among the Orthodox community of one set of *mitzvot* from the other.

The precepts between man and Creator are generally expressed and contained within an unchanging formula, unaffected by the varying activities that emerge from the changing texture of desires of society in general and the individual in particular. Prayer, Shabbat and Tefillin are, to a great extent, a private communication between the observer and G-d, without infringement from external distractions. Yet, even within this area of supposed competence, we find evidence of alienation and division among observant Jews.

A story is told of a conversation that took place between the Besht (Baal Shem Tov) and a congregant. Following a service, the Besht approached the congregant and extended the greeting of *Shalom Aleichem* (peace be unto you). The hassid was taken aback at this, and asked the Besht why he had used this form of greeting, since he surely knew that the law obliged one to use it only if one had not seen a friend for three days or more. "You know, Rabbi" he continued, "that I have never left this town for as much as a single day, and attend morning and evening services here every day, as is required of every devout Jew. So why the greeting?"

"All this is undoubtedly true, my son," replied the Besht, "I do see you every day. However, I should like to know where you are while you are sitting in meditation; it seems to me that your mind, soul and thoughts are elsewhere, perhaps comtemplating some new business venture. Placing the *tefillin* on your hand and head for so many years, day after day has become an automatic habit, apparently exerting little influence over the content of your thoughts and meditations. I therefore extended to you a greeting upon your return from your place of business."

The lack of unity and focus illustrated by this story is merely a symptom of a more widespread disease, namely the continuing separation between ritual and social commandments. We are enjoined to carry out both; each when properly observed leads to appreciation and observance of the other, so that over-emphasis on either is an indication of lack of understanding of the whole. The ritual *mitzvot,* if carried out in their true spirit and understanding, ought to lead to greater charity to one's neighbour, just as the *mitzvot* between man and man ought to lead to a realisation of the omnipresence and omnipotence of the Creator, and thence to a desire to celebrate His greatness. The goal of *Devekuth,* which is the goal not of one set of *mitzvot* nor of the other, but of both taken and practiced together, can only be pursued through a true understanding of the essential unity of the Torah. Only when that unity has been realised can a true love of one's neighbour come into being.

CHAPTER XII

A CONTEMPLATION

Although the knowledge of Kabbalah is discussed and encased in many volumes of writing, both ancient and modern, it should not be thought that its teachings are contained solely in the written word. In previous chapters we have shown that Kabbalah lies at the very heart of the system of holy actions and deeds known as *mitzvot;* without these actions, the life of a Jew is considered incomplete and lacking. However, inner devotion is also an important element of Jewish teaching, and this aspect, too, is emphasised by the teaching of Kabbalah.

The need to centre one's inner world with the intention appropriate to the situation is known in Hebrew as *Kavannah,* or Direction. While this meditation and the fulfillment of mitzvot are essentially inseparable, we feel that many Jews who may read this book, and who have grown up without knowing the taste of mitzvot, will benefit from a contemplation to help link the teachings of Kabbalah with their application in the world of action.

A generation has arisen which, being aware of its Jewishness, does not know how to express that aspect of its identity. There is, however, a widespread awareness of the need for inner sincerity and wholeness, which may not find satisfaction in the contemporary teachings of Judaism. For this reason, it seems fitting to close this book with a contemplation which, although no substitute for the performance of *mitzvot,* will, it is hoped, arouse in the reader a deeper appreciation of the intentions of this book, and allow him or her a further insight into the workings and significance of the teachings of Kabbalah.

R. Abba was one day discussing the teachings of Torah with the Sacred Lamp (R. Shimon bar Yohai).[110] "Why is it," he asked R. Shimon, "that, from all the people of the world, only the Jews always sway back and forth when they are studying Torah, an action that seems to come naturally to them, so that they cannot keep still?"

R. Shimon replied, "Alas for mankind who wander about like cattle without any understanding. This matter alone is enough to distinguish the holy souls of Israel from the souls of heathen people. The souls of Israel were cut from the Holy Lamp, as it is written, 'The spirit of man is the lamp of the Lord' (Proverbs XX,27). Once this lamp has been lit from the supernal Torah, its light never stops moving for an instant, like the flame of a wick that is never still. Thus when one of the Children of Israel pronounces a single word of Torah, a light is kindled and he is unable to keep still; thus he sways backwards and forwards like the wick of a candle. The souls of heathens, however, are like stubble, which when it burns, has no flame; thus they remain motionless, like wood that burns without a flame."

Elsewhere in the Zohar[111], we find a discussion of the two verses of Torah, "For the Lord thy G-d is a consuming fire" (Deut.IV,24), and "But ye that did cleave unto the Lord your G-d are alive every one of you this day" (Deut.IV,4). The apparent contradiction in these words is explained by R. Shimon: "It has already been established.,.,.,. that there is a fire which consumes fire and destroys it, there being fires of different grades of strength. If we extend this concept, we might say that anyone wishing to penetrate the mystery of the holy unity should contemplate the flame that rises from a burning coal or candle.

The flame cannot rise unless it is attached to some physical substance. Furthermore, within the flame itself there are to be found two lights: one is white and luminous, the other black, or blue. The white light is the more elevated of the two and ascends steadily. The black or blue light is beneath and acts as a pedestal for the white light. The two are inseperably joined to one another, with the white light resting and enthroned upon the blue. The blue lower flame is itself attached to something physical beneath it, which feeds it and makes it join with the white flame above. Sometimes the blue light may become red in colour, but the white light above never changes. Thus the lower light, which is either blue or red, forms a connection between the white light above amid the physical substance below, which keeps it alight. The nature of this lower light is to destroy anything that is beneath it or in contact with it; it is the source of destruction and death. The white light above it, however, neither consumes nor destroys, nor does it ever change.,.,. This is why Moses said, 'For the Lord thy G-d is a consuming fire', meaning that He consumes all that is beneath Him — 'thy G-d' and not 'our G-d', because Moses had reached the level of the upper white light, which does not consume or destroy.

By transgressing the Lord's Commandments, the Children of Israel have placed themselves in the realm of the judgement of the lower blue flame, whose nature is destruction; but those who obeyed the Holy Commandments, thereby 'cleaving to the Lord thy G-d', attached themselves to the upper white flame, whose nature is constant, unchanging, and beyond the realms of destruction. Thus there are different grades of fire, some higher and some lower. There are different aspects to the flame of a coal or candle: that which is attached to the physical realm, draws its life from the physical and ultimately destroys it, and that which is above the realm of destruction is preserved.

"Now observe", continues R. Shimon: "The motivating force by which the blue flame is kindled, and by which it becomes attached to the white light, comes only from Israel, who cleave to it from beneath. Now, although the nature of the blue light is to consume everything that comes into contact with it from below, Israel can cleave to it from beneath without being destroyed, as it is written, 'But ye that did cleave to the Lord your G-d are alive every one of the you this day'. It is written 'Your G-d' and not 'Our G-d', indicating the blue flame that destroys all with which it comes into contact from below. Yet you (Israel) cleave to it and are still alive. Above the white light and surrounding it is yet another light, which can hardly by seen and which symbolises the Supreme Essence. Thus the ascending flame is a symbol of the most elevated mysteries of wisdom".

The three elements that we can observe in the flame — the wick, the blue light and the white light — symbolise the three elements of man's spirit, and refer to the three columns we have discussed throughout this book. The white light represents the right column, the Desire to Impart; this is the moral strength which constantly strives to ascend to and unite with the Absolute. While it burns it does not consume, acting rather as an illuminating vehicle permeated with light through which one can become one with the eternal source of light, the Creator.

The blue or black flame symbolises the left column, the Desire to Receive, and is characterised by its connection with the physical body. It constantly draws up energy from that which is beneath it, and represents the aspect of man that seeks to deny spirituality, pursuing material pleasures for himself alone. Finally, the wick represents the synthesizing and unifying force of both the blue and the clear white flame, which is the central column.

How can Israel, the wick of the candle, exist without being destroyed by the "consuming fire" of the blue flame? By the very fact, says the Zohar, that Israel, unlike the candle, was created from the Holy Lamp, whose power and energy are infinite and inexhaustible. If we draw only on the energy of the physical world, as the wick draws its energy from the body of the candle, that energy will, in time, be exhausted by the fire of the left column, the Desire to Receive. If, however, we connect with the limitless energy of the Creator, through a true understanding of the teachings of Torah and a fulfillment of mitzvot, then we shall have transcended the destroying influence of the blue flame, and can connect with the unchanging purity of the clear white flame above. As we have stressed repeatedly throughout this book, this unity is not a negation of the left column, any more than the candle can burn without the blue flame. The choice facing us is whether to cut ourselves off from that endless source of energy and be consumed by the devouring fire of the Desire to Receive, or to connect with our birthright and cleave to G-d without being destroyed.

The teachings of Kabbalah are not merely concerned, therefore, with theoretical descriptions of the structure of the universe. They are primarily concerned with preparing man for knowledge of the Almighty through direct awareness of the physical world, and through intuitive connections brought about by a deep contemplation of the relationships between upper and lower worlds.

BIOGRAPHICAL NOTES

Aaron ha-Levy — (c. 1234-1300) Barcelona, known for his work, Sefer ha-Hinukh (Book of Education); Student of Nahmamides.

Aaron Berekiah ben Moses of Modena — (1600), Italian Kabbalist famous for his "Ma'avar Yabok" (Crossing the Yabok), one of the most profound concepts in Kabbalah.

Abarbanel, R. Don Isaac - (b. Lisbon 1437, d, Venice 1509). Prediscovered the wondrous world of the mystical realm in general and the Kabbalah in particular. Served the Spanish royal house before the expulsion of the Jews from Spain. He succeeded in piercing the iron curtain concealing the mysterious enigmas of redemption cloaked in the Book of Daniel. He offered encouragement to Jews following their expulsion from Spain by composing several works concerned with the central desire of that period, the coming of the Messiah.

Abba, R., — (circa 130A.D.) Student of R. Shimon Bar Yohai who, according to the Zohar (III, P.287b) actually put into writing the words of the Zohar as they were revealed by R. Shimon Bar Yohai.

Abbaye (circa 270 c.e. — 339). One of the most prominent Amoraim; together with his opponent Rava mentioned most often in discourses in the Babylonian Talmud.

Abraham, Partriarch, (1900 B.C.E.) — considered to be the chariot of the Sefirah Hesed (Kindness), as exemplified in the Book of Genesis.

Abraham ben David — see Rabad

Abraham ben Eliezer ha-Levy Beruchim — (c. 1515-1593) Kabbalist born in Morocco and later settled in Safed where he joined first the school of R. Moses Cordovero and then R. Isaac Lurias' circle.

Abraham ben Eliezer ha-Levi (c. 1450-1530) Spanish Kabbalist known for his "Masoret ha-Hokmah" (Transmission of the Wisdom) who after the expulsion of the Jews from Spain settled in Jerusalem.

Abraham ben Isaac (Gerondi) (C. 13th century) famous Spanish Kabbalist whose Kabbalistic hymns and prayers are widely known. "Ahot Ketannah" (Little Sister) his most famous prayer recited before the Rosh Hashona prayers describes the exile of the Jewish people or more specifically "Galut ha-Shekinah."

Abraham ben Isaac of Narbonne — (c.1110-1179), Talmudist and Rabbi of Provence whose famous work, Sefer ha-Eshkol, was the primary work of codification of halacha, which served as a model for subsequent codifications. Father-in-law of Abraham ben David of Posquieres, the Rabad.

Abraham ben Israel of Brody — (1749-1836) famed Italian Kabbalist known for his extreme piety and fasting. Author of many Kabbalistic works.

Abraham ben Moses ben Maimon (1186-1237) — Son of Maimonides, scholar and subsequent leader of the Egyptian Jewish community following the death of his father. After the great controversy erupted in Provence and Spain over the writings of his father, he came to his fathers defense. While Maimonides directed all his efforts to codifying the Talmud, his sons' view of Judaism was of a mystical nature.

Abulafia-Abraham ben Samuel (c. 1240-1290) Kabbalist of Spain and Italy. He considered himself the representative of prophetic Kabbalah.

Aderet, Solomon ben Abraham (c.b. 1235 Barcelona -d 1310) Also known as the RASHBA, acronym for his full name, famous for his talmudical commentaries, poetry, philosophy and lesser known for his Kabbalistic writings. Student of R. Jonah Gerondi and Nahmanides.

Akiva, R. Ben Joseph — (c 15-135A.D.) — younger contemporary of Rabbi Gamliel; teacher of Rabbi Shimon Bar Yohai, the author of the Zohar (Book of Splendor); began the study of the Torah at the age of forty, motivated by his wife Rachel, the daughter of the wealthy Kalba Shevua by whom he was employed as a shepherd (Tractate Ketubot, P. 62b.). One of the most prominent leaders- (Tanna), his disciples in his academy at Bene Berak numbered some twenty-four thousand (Tractate Sanhedrin 32A); he compiled and systemized the topics of Torah Bal Peh (Talmud) known as the Mishnah of Rabbi Akiba (Mishnah, Tractate Sanhedrin 3). This work laid the foundation for the final compilation of the Mishna by Rabbi Jehudah ha-Nasi (the Prince). Main supporter of Bar Kochba whom he considered to be the Messiah, in the latter's insurrection against Rome; captured by the Romans and put to death for studying Torah, expiring with the Shema upon his lips."With the passing of Rabbi Akiva, the crown of the Torah ceased to exist" (Tractate Sotah 92).

Alkabetz, R. Shlomo Halevi (b. 1505-Solonica, d. 1576 Safed) Kabbalist and mystical poet, author of L'cha Dodi recited Friday evening, founder of the famous Kabbalistic centre at Salonica. He was a contemporary of R. Joseph Caro, author of the Shulchan Aruch and the Ari, R. Isaac Luria.

Alshikh, R. Moses (b. 1508-d.1600 Damascus), most important homiletician of the 16th century, contemporary of R. Joseph Karo and the Ari. R. Isaac Luria. Member of the Rabbinical Council in Safed, wrote an allegorical-mystical Bible commentary.

Ari — See R. Yitzhak (Isaac) Luria.

Ashlag, R. Yehuda — (1886-1955) Famed Kabbalist known as the pioneer of modern Kabbalism, developed a new approach to the understanding of the Lurianic system. His profound yet accessible writings provided the necessary keys in comprehending the Zohar. His translation of the entire **Zohar,** known as the Sulam, facilitated the widespread interest of this sublime and obstruse text. He opened the portals to spiritual Judaism through his sixteen volume textbook called "The Study of the Ten Luminous Emanations."

Attar, R. Hayyim (b.1696 Morocco d. 1743 Jerusalem). Kabbalist who became famous for his best known and important commentary on the Bible, Or Ha-Hayyim (Light of Life), based entirely on Kabbalistic teachings. In 1741, settled in Jerusalem and established an academy of learning. His yarzeit is celebrated by many thousands of Jews each year in Jerusalem.

Azulai, R. Abraham Ben Mordchai, (1570-1643) famous Kabbalist born in Fez from a family of Kabbalists of Castilian origin, wrote three treatises on the Zohar; Or Levanah (Light of the Moon), Or ha-Chamah (Light of the Sun), and Or-ha-Ganuz (the Hidden Light), based primarily on the Lurianic system. Underscored the permission granted for *all* to enter the gates of the world of mysticism.

Azulai, R. Haim Yosef David (b.1724 Jerusalem-d. 1806 Leghorn). Known by his Hebrew acronym "HIDA". Kabbalist, halachist and historian, authored the famous bibliographic work Shem-Hagedolim.

Baal Shem- see Israel baal Shem Tov

Bahir (Sefer ha-Bahir)- the book Bahir together with the Zohar was widely known in thirteenth century Spain. Authorship attributed to R. Nehunia ben ha-Kana. As the Zohar means "splendor", so this work "Bahir" means "brightness". Contains interpretations of letters and sounds, parables and mystical ideas linked to the Torah, following the profound explanations of the Zohar.

Bahya ben Asher ben Hlava (13th century Spanish kabbalist famous for his commentary on the Bible and numerous works on the

Kabbalah, disciple of Solomon b. Abraham Aderet.

Bahya, R. Ibn Pakuda — (c.1080-1170) Kabbalist and philosopher who lived in Spain, author of the famous work Havot ha-levavot (Duties of the Heart).

Barzillai, Judah ben Al-Bargeloni — 12th century Spanish Kabbalist and halachist known for his commentary on the Sefer Yetzirah called Perush Sefer Yetzirah. His other works include Sefer ha-Ittim, which deals with the Jewish festivals which are referred to extensively by later commentaries.

Ben Azzai — (c.130) a younger contemporary of Rabbi Akiba. The Talmud and Zohar says "Four persons entered the *Pardes* (Orchard), concerning the nature and process of creation. These were: Ben Azzai, Ben Zoma, Aher (another, the surname given to Elisha Ben Abuyah) and R. Akiba. Ben Azzai, Ben Zoma and Aher entered the domains of p'shat (simple), *remez* (hint), *drush* (homiletical) interpretations of the Torah. R. Akiba entered the domain of Sod (Kabbalah), and he alone survived. (Zohar I, P. 26b and tractate Hagigah, P.14b). Ben Zoma said, "Who is wise? He that learns from all men, as it is written." From all my teachers have I gained knowledge. (Psalms 119:99).

Ben ha-Kanah — see Nehunya Ben ha-kanah

Ben Zakai — see Johanan R.

Botarel, Moses ben Isaac —15th century Spanish kabbalist, whose main work is a commentary on the Sefer Yetzirah. This invaluable work stemmed from his desire to enhance the status of Kabbalism.

Brandwein, R. Yehuda Zvi (1904-1969), Kabbalist and significant student of rabbi Ashlag. His vast knowledge of the Lurianic system enabled him to codify and edit the entire writings of the Ari, R. Yitzchak Luria. Continued with the similar style of translation and commentary of Rabbi Ashlag known as "Maalot ha-Sulam (Extension of the Ladder) on those works of R.

Shimon Bar Yohai, which R. Ashlag didn't complete during his lifetime, namely Hashmotot ha-Zohar (Various other Writings) and Tikune Zohar (Addendum to the Zohar). First Jewish settler within the Old City of Jerusalem after the Six day War.

Cordovero, R. Moses (1522-1570) — also known by the abbreviation REMAK, famed Kabbalist of Safeds' "golden age", brother-in-law of R. Shlomo Alkabetz, and one-time teacher of the Ari, R. Luria. His large main work "Ohr Yakar", (Precious Light), on the entire Zohar has only recently begun to see the light of day. Originator of one of the two basic systems of understanding the Zohar. His other major work 'Pardes Remmonim' (Garden of Pomegranates) is a systematic compendium of Kabbalistic concepts surrounding the internal action of the original unified energy force emanating from the Creator. R. Haim Vital, student of R. Yitzchak Luria, had a dream in which the Remak revealed to him, that in the age of the Messiah the Lurianic system would prevail.

Crescas, Hasdai — (b.1340 Barcelona-d.1412 Zaragoza) — famed Spanish Kabbalist and philosopher whose criticism of Jewish Aristotelianism provided a stimulus for and paved the way to an in depth recognition of the internal, metaphysical world of reality. His main work was "Or-Adonai (The Light of G-d) in which he presented his criticism of Jewish Aristotelianism.

De Leon, Moses — See Leon, Moses De

Donolo Shabbatai (c.913-982) famed Italian Kabbalist and physician who was born in Oria, Italy. His most famous work on Kabbalah is his book "Sefer Hakhmoni", a commentary on the Sefer Yetzirah. His Sefer Ha-Mirkahot (Book of Remedies) drew material from his knowledge of "Hakarot Hapartzuf" (physiognomies) and astrology, which undoubtedly was based on his comprehension of the Kabbalah. His Sefer Hakhmoni provides a massive collection of information regarding the study of astronomy; without it, the study of astrology would remain incomprehensible.

Eleazar ben Judah, Rabbi of Worms (c.1176 Speyer-d.1238 Worms) pupil of R. Judah ben Samuel, the Pious. His work "Rokeah" presents a concept of mysticism relating to moral practice.

Elijah ben Solomon — see the "Gaon of Vilna"

Elisha ben Abuyah — entered the Pardes and became heretical, known as *Aher* ("that other one").

Galante, R. Abraham (c. 1570) — famed Safed Kabbalist of the sixteenth century, known for his commentary on the Zohar.

Galico, R. Elisha — famed Kabbalist of the sixteenth century, known for his commentary on the Zohar. Member of the Rabbinical Court of R. Yosef Karo in Safed.

Gaon of Vilna — (1720-1797) ha-Gaon R. Eliyahu (abreviated ha-Gra), famous for his Kabbalistic writings which number some eighty volumes, halachist of the Talmud.

Gerondi, R. Moses ben Solomon D'escola (b. 1244, Gerona-d. 1263 Toledo) Cousin of Nahmanides, famous for ethical writings, "Shaarei Teshuvah" and "Sefer ha-Yira".

Gikatila, R. Joseph (c.1270)- famed Spanish Kabbalist whose writings Ginnath Egoz (Garden of Nut Trees), Iggereth ha-Kodesh (Holy Letter) and Shaare Orah (Gates of Light) provided a systematic development to the internal structure and meaning of symbolism.

Hayim, R. Kohen (c.1600) famed Kabbalist of Aleppo, student of R. Hayim Vital, composer of mystical hymns in the form of dialogues between the Creator and Israel.

Hayim Vital, R.- (b.1543 Safed-d. Damascus 1620) the selected student of R. Isaac Luria, the Ari, who together with his son

Shmuel accepted the task of recording the Ari's thoughts on paper.

Ibn Gaon, Shem Tov ben Abraham (late 13th to 14th centuries), Spanish Kabbalist and halakhist whose teacher was Solomon ben Abraham Aderet. His best known work on the Kabbalah is "Keter Shem Tov" and "Migdal Oz", a commentary on the Mishneh Torah of Maimonindes.

Ibn Habib, Jacob ben Solomon (c.1440-1515) Rabbinical scholar born in Castile, Spain; heading a yeshivah which was one of the largest in Spain. On the expulsion of the Jews from Spain he went to Portugal and then on to Salonika, which had become the main centre for the study of Kabbalah. His most famous work, Ein Yakov, in which he assembled the aggadot of the Babylonian and Jerusalem Talmud.

Ibn Motot, Samuel ben Saadiah (c.1370) Spanish Kabbalist and was one of the inner circle of Spanish Kabbalists in Castile.

Ibn Shem Tov, Shem Tov (c.1380-1440) Spanish Kabbalist, known as the anti-Maimonidean Kabbalist.

Ibn Waqar, Joseph ben Abraham (c.14th Century) Kabbalist who lived in Toledo, Spain and formulated his Kabbalistic ideas through his now famous poem, Shir ha-Yihud.

Isaac ben Todros of Barcelona — 14th century Spanish Kabbalist and student of Nahmanides whose teachings are included among the writings of the disciples of Nahmanides.

Isaac the Blind — (c.1200) famous Spanish Kabbalist who lived in Provence, son of the famed Kabbalist, Rabbi Abraham ben David of Posquieres.

Ishmael, R. ben Elisha — famous Tanna of the first and second centuries, c.e., contemporary of Rabbi Akiba and among the martyrs of the Hadrian persecution in 135c.e. He won for himself a permanent place as a figure in Jewish mysticism with his explanations of the twenty two letters of the Hebrew alphabet as described in his "Baraita de R. Ishmael". He also authored Thirteen Principles of Logic.

Israel Baal-Shem Tov (1700-1760) also known as "BeSHT" (abbreviation of Baal Shem Tov) the founder of hasidism. The light of his teaching and his holy wisdom is based on the foundations of the Ari, R. Isaac Luria. The "BeSHT" passed on his teachings only by word of mouth. However, the internal strength of his teachings represented for the average Jew of Eastern Europe the opportunity of reaching endless heights of spiritual development with the help of Kabbalistic Kavanot. "The act of 'devekut'," (communion with the Almighty), remarked the BeSHT, "can best be achieved by man through joy and the proper relationship to his fellow man, and that the Creator, the source of internal energy and strength dwell within us at all times, and what is left to man is to reveal and activate this potential energy."

Jacob ben Jacob, Ha-Kohen (c.13th century) famed Kabbalist of the communities in Provence and Spain. Various works on Kabbalah have been attributed to him, however, without certainty.

Johanan Ben Zakai, R. (c50A.D.) youngest disciple of Hillel who foresaw the destruction of the Temple (Tractate Yuma 39b), concluded that the establishment of a Torah centre was the last and only hope for the Jews to exist as a nation without the binding force of the Holy Temple. Was smuggled out of Jerusalem as a corpse by his students R. Eliezer ben Hyrcanus and R. Joshua ben Hananiah, and presented himself before the Roman commander Vespasian asking his permission to establish a Torah academy in Yavneh. (Tractate Gitin 55b.) His request granted, Yavneh became the spiritual centre of Jewish life where the Great Sanhedrin was reestablished.

Joseph Ibn Shraga — famed 15th century Italian Kabbalist

Joseph Ibn-Tabul — Kabbalist living in Safed (c.16th century) who taught the Lurianic system of Kabbalah.

Judah ben Kalonymus ben Moses of Mainz — 13th century Kabbalist and halachic authority whose teacher in mysticism was Judah ben Samuel ha-Hasid.

Judah ben Samuel ha-Hasid (c1150-1217) who lived in Regensburg. Although known for his work Sefer Hasidim, he was the teacher of many subsequent Kabbalists among whom were his grandson, Eleazar b. Moses ha Darshon, and his great grandson, Moses ben Eleazar.

Karo, R. Joseph (b.1488 Spain-d. 1575 Safed) — author of the "Shulkhan Arukh" the most authoritative codification of Jewish law, and great Rabbinical authority of the sixteenth century. Also known for his Kabbalistic writing "Magid Meshurim" which contains visions and revelations only attributable to a Kabbalist.

Leon R. Moses de -ben Shemtov (c.1290) Famed Kabbalist in Spain who revealed for the first time the existence of a physical instrument that can provide spiritual insights to the five books of Moses, the Zohar (Book of Splendor), the main work of Kabbalistic literature.

Levi, R. Isaac of Berdichev — (1740-1809) famous Hasidic Master whose constant use of the expression "Derbarmdiger Gott" (Merciful Lord), he was known as the "Derbarmdiger" for his principles: love of the Lord and love of his fellow man.

Loew, R. Judah ben Bezalel — see Maharal

Luria, R. Yitzhak — (b.1534 Jerusalem-d. 1572 Safed). Known as the "Ari," the "Lion" or "Ari Hakodesh", the Holy Lion, founder of the Lurianic system of Kabbalah.

Luzzatto, R. Moshe Hayim (b.1707, Padua-d. 1746 Tiberias) Also known by the acronym "RAMHAL." Kabbalist and Poet, author of the Book, "The One Hundred Thirty Eight Openings to the Kabbalah." and his ethical religious work, Mesillat Yesharim ("Paths of the Upright").

Maharal, Loew, R. Judah ben Bezalel (1525-1609) the Great Rabbi Loew, abbreviated as 'MaHaRaL', had earned a reputation as a performer of miralces and famed for his Kabbalistic writings: "Beer ha-Golah", "Netivot Olam," and "Tiferet Israel."

Maimonides-Rabbi Moses Ben Maimon (b.1135 Cordoba-d.1204 Fostat) (buried in Tiberias) known by the Acronym RaMBaM. Born in Cordova, Spain, Maimonides was forced to emigrate, at first to Morocco, then to Egypt where he earned his living practicing medicine. His Mishnah Torah (Copy of the Law) was the first systematic exposition of Jewish Law. His "articles of faith", are quoted in most Jewish prayer books. Most important Jewish philosopher of the Middle ages. His thoughts strongly influenced all philosophical thinking of his era through his main philosophical work 'Morah Nevukhim", (Guide for the Perplexed). Also "Yad ha-Hazakah" (Strong Hand) is a restructuring of the whole content of Biblical Law.

Meir-Enlightener — second century "Tanna" and one of the most prominent disciples of Rabbi Akiba. One of the five surviving students who did not perish in the great plague of Roman bestiality in the death of Rabbi Akiba's 24,000 students. His work in systemizing the Halakhah laid the foundation of the present Mishnah. He was the husband of the famous Beruria, daughter of the martyred Rabbi Hananiah ben Tradion.

Menahem Azariah of Fano — (c.1609), famous Italian Kabbalist whose work "Ma'amar ha-Nefesh" follows the mystical idea developed by R. Yitzchak Luria concerning the soul, in that each letter of the Torah represents the upper root of the soul of each individual in Israel. Consequently, each individual soul has its own framework of reference in understanding the Torah.

Midrash Rabbah (research, homiletical interpretation) denoting the oldest Amoraic work following the revelation of the Zohar to R. Shimon Bar Yohai. Contains collections of interpretations, homiletical discourses and poetic reflections of the Torah by "Tannaim and Amoraim."

Midrash ha-Ne'elam collection of dialogues and lectures between R. Shimon Bar Yohai and his pupils, included within the main body of the Zohar. However, these sections under the topical caption "Midrash ha Ne'elam" are considerably more difficult and abstruse than the main body of this work.

Minyan — (number) — the minimum number of participants needed to execute and effect a maximum structure of "D'vekut" (Communion) with the source factor, namely the Creator, who is the source of all positive energy. Since any complete and totally efficient structure (more specifically concerning communications) is comprised of the Ten Sefirot, consequently, the ten individuals, each one representing an aspect of the Ten Sefirot must be present to effect maximum communion, or connection. The preference for male participants as opposed to the female simply projects the concept of the necessity for positive channeling represented by the male. The female, whose internal structure is one of negative channeling, (negative not to be misunderstood as being inferior or wrong but similar to the negative wire in our electrical system, which actually is the primary source of energy) and because of her superior internal composition, prayer, which provides positive energy, would be redundant in as much as the female does not require the participation in a minyan due to her *constant* connection to energy.

Mishnah — (repetition) essence of the oral interpretation of the Torah, canonical collection of writings of the Tannaim, edited and compiled in the second century by R. Judah ha-Nasi.

Mishnah Torah — Deuteronomy, the fifth book of the Torah. See also Maimonides.

Mitzvah — (precept of the Torah) which was placed at the disposal of the Jew, to provide him with the metaphysical communication system needed to connect with the Creator for internal energy.

Moses, R. ben Jacob (c.1440-1520). Talmudic scholar and Kabbalist who lived in Lithuania. Famous for his commentary "Ozar ha-Shem" on the Sefer Yetzirah and Shushan Sodot dealing with cryptic writing.

Moses ben Maimon — See Maimonides
Moses ben Nahman — See Nahmanides
Moses ben Shem Tov de Leon — see Leon

Moses, R. ben Solomon of Burgos (c.1230-1300) a leading Kabbalist in Spain, student of Jacob ben Jacob ha-Kohen of Provence.

Nahmanides — (**R. Moses ben Nahman:** abbreviated RaMBAN)-born Gerona 1195-d.1270 Akko. Famed Spanish Kabbalist, Talmudic scholar and biblical exegete who adopted a mystical position in the battle which raged around philosophy during the thirteenth century. His commentary on the Sefer Yetzira provides an in-depth comprehension to this abstruse and difficult work on the Kabbalah. His commentary on the Bible cannot be understood apart from a comprehension of the Kabbalah. His opposition to Aristotelianism, which had endangered the very foundations of Judaism in Spain, was completely based on the principal doctrines of the Zohar, which legend relates was already known to Nahmanides. The mysteries of the Kabbalah which initially took hold during the latter half of the twelfth century in Provence and subsequently came to full bloom there and in Northern Spain in the thirteenth century was the Creator's beneficience for a reawakening and rebirth of a new life under its influence. Nahmanides played no small role in this new development if not possibly the harbinger of this movement which climaxed a period in the history of the Jews on which they have always looked back with pride when referring to this "Golden Age in Spain".

Najara, R. Moses (c.16th century) Kabbalist who lived in Safed and studied within the school of the Lurianic system. Author of several works on the Kabbalah.

Nathan ha-Babli, R. (c.170c.e) An older contemporary of R. Judah ha-Nasi of the Talmudic period, author of a parallel work to the Tractate Ethics of the Fathers which is a homiletical exposition of Abot of the Fathers.

Nehemia ben Hakanah, R. (c.70-130 c.e.) A student of R. Johanan ben Zakkai (Baba Batra 10a). A famed mystic and author of "Ana B'Koah" a recitation included in the morning prayer. This profound mystical prayer is connected with and related to the Seven Sefirot in as much as each of the seven sentences relate to a particular Sefirah. This prayer is also included in the counting of the Omer with its significance being the mystical relationship to each day of the forty-nine days that commence with the second day of Passover and end the day before Shevuot. Since the cosmological influence during this period is considered to be totally negative and destructive, the Ari, R. Isaac Luria, explains in his "Book of Meditation", the use of this prayer in altering the Cosmic influence of these forty-nine days. He has also been considered the author of the famed Kabbalistic text, the "Sefer Bahir."

Obadiah ben Abraham Bertinoro — (c.b. 1430 Italy-d. 1525 Jerusalem) Famous for his commentary on the Mishnah.

Pardes (Orchard) — refers to the four levels of interpretation. Each consonant of the words PaRDeS indicates one of the levels. The letter P stands for Peshat, the simple, literal meaning. The letter R for Remez, hint or allegorical interpretation, D for Drash, the homiletical and S for Sod, the inner, Kabbalistic meaning. See also ben Azzai.

Pinchas ben Yair — Tannah of the first Century and father-in law of R. Shimon Bar Yohai.

Pirke de Rabbi Eliezer — 1st midrashic work on Bereshit and parts of Shemot: ascribed to Rabbi Eliezer ben Hyrcanus. Disciple of R. Johanan ben Zakkai whom he helped smuggle out of Jerusalem. Also known as R. Eliezer ha-Gadol (Tractate Sotah 9). Avot de R. Nathan (25,3) records that R. Akiba applied to R. Eliezer the remarks that Elisha had applied to Elijah the Prophet (Kings 2:12) "Oh my father, the chariot of Israel and the horsemen thereof". His revelation of "He and His Name is one", describing the World of En Sof, is probably the most remarkable and profound description known.

Poppers, Meir ben Judah Loeb Ha-Kohen — 17th century Kabbalist, pupil of Jacob Zemah and one of the final editors of Hayim Vital's writings of the Kitvey Ari (writings of the Ari). He wrote extensively according to the Lurianic system.

Rabad (R. Abraham ben David: known by his acronym 'RABD'), of Poquieres (c.1125-1198) Kabbalistic and Talmudic authority who lived in Provence. A distinguished authoritative scholar known for his in-depth criticism of Maimonides, produced numerous literary works, Torat ha-Bayit and Ba-al Hanefesh to mention a few. His commentary on the Sefer Yetzirah is of special significance, in as much as this work established the Rabad as one of the most prominent figures in Kabbalistic literature. This work (and his probing into the metaphysical strata of Kabbalah) exerted considerable influence on subsequent Spanish Kabbalists. He defined heretofore abstract concepts with a maximum of clarity. For this he attained for himself a special place in history as one of the greatest commentators on the Kabbalah.

Radbaz — see Zimra, David ben RaDBaZ

Rashba — see Aderet, Solomon ben Abraham

Recanati, R. Menahem ben Benyamin — (c. 1350 — 1440) Italian Kabbalist, whose family originally came from Spain. . . His main Kabbalistic work was Perush ol ha-Torah (commentary on the Torah), and Ta'amai ha-Mitzvot (Explanation of the precepts). He is quoted extensively throughout the writings of the Ari, R. Isaac Luria. The Ari, mentioning "The Sefer ha-Recanati", tells of an incident where a person, who, on the night of Hoshana Rabba — which according to the Zohar, is the time when we can know if our sins have been purified and we shall live for another year — went out at midnight according to the teachings of the Ari. Upon seeing that his full shadow didn't appear and the head was missing, he knew this was a sign that he needed to attain a higher degree of purity. He returned to the house of study and wept and repented wholeheartedly and when he felt cleaner inside he went outside again and observed that his prayers had been accepted as he saw his full shadow by the light of the moon.*
*Gate of Meditation P. 307b.

Saadia ben Joseph Gaon — (882-942), born in Egypt, author, scholar, Kabbalist of the gaonic period and leader of Babylonian Jewry. His original commentary on the Sefer Yetzirah was written in Arabic and translated into Hebrew. His principal work was "Emunot ve-Daot" (Doctrines and opinions).

Saba, Abraham ben Jacob (c. 1500), Spanish Kabbalist and exegete, who settled in Portugal after the expulsion of the Jews from Spain. When forced conversion of Jews was decreed in Portugal in 1497 he left for Fez in Morocco. Known for his famed work on the Bible "Zeror ha-Mor", and "Perush Eser-Sefirot" (Explanation of the Ten Sefirot).

Sahula, Isaac ben Solomon Abi (c. 1240) scholar and Kabbalist who lived in the town of Guadalajara in Castile. Was a student of the famed Kabbalist Moses of Burgos and acquaintance of Moses ben Shem Tov de Leon.

Sahula, Meir ben Solomon Abi (c. 1250-1335), Spanish Kabbalist and younger brother of Isaac Abi Sahula who lived in Guadalajara which was then a centre of Kabbalistic learning. Famous for his commentary of the "Sefer Yetzirah" and "Sefer ha-Bahir."

Samuel Vital — (c. 1598-1678), Kabbalist, son of Hayim Vital, considered among the important Talmudic authorities of Damascus, re-edited his fathers writings which the Ari, R. Isaac Luria transmitted orally.

Sefer ha-Bahir — see Bahir

Sharabi, Shalom (1720-1777) Kabbalist born in Yemen, emigrated to Palestine and studied at the Kabbalistic yeshivah Bet El in Jerusalem. As a Jerusalem Kabbalist, he studied the Lurianic system of Kabbalah; his works are on Lurianic Kabbalah. Particularly famous is his Nehar Shalom, which includes the secrets and meditations on prayer and mitzvot.

Shaloh-R. Isaiah ben Abraham Horowitz (1565-1630) Kabbalist, author of Shenai Lukot ha-Brit (The two Tablets of the Covenant) also known by the acronym "Shaloh".

Shimon ha-Tsadik — member of the Sanhedrin and High Priest of the Second temple.

Solomon Aderet — see Aderet, Solomon

Tannaim — meaning teachers of the oral law during the first to the third centuries, which is the framework of the Mishna.

Vital — see Hayim Vital

Vital, Joseph — 15th century scribe, especially known for his preciseness in writing tephillin which were known as Tefillin of the Rabbi of Calabria. Father of Hayim Vital.

Vital, Moses ben Joseph — Younger brother of Hayim Vital and active in the Kabbalistic circle of Safed.

Vital, Samuel — see Samuel Vital

Yosi ben Jacob — one of the ten students of R. Shimon Bar Yohai who left his body during the Greater Assembly.

Zacuto, Moses ben Mordecai (c. 1620-1697), Kabbalist and poet. He was born into a Portuguese Marrano family in Amsterdam. Zacuto published exoteric works in addition to his numerous writings on the Kabbalah.

Zemah, Jacob ben Hayim — famed 17th century Kabbalist, born in Portugal, settled in Safed where he took up the study of Kabbalah in the Lurianic tradition. Author of many works on the Zohar as well as Lurianic concepts and customs.

Zimra, David ben (b.1479 — Spain, d.1573 Safed). Exiled from Spain at age 13, and moved to Safed. In 1512 went to Egypt, where he became spiritual leader until 1569 when he returned to Safed. His distinguished student during his stay in Egypt was the Ari, R. Isaac Luria.

APPENDIX I

Stages of Emanation and Creation

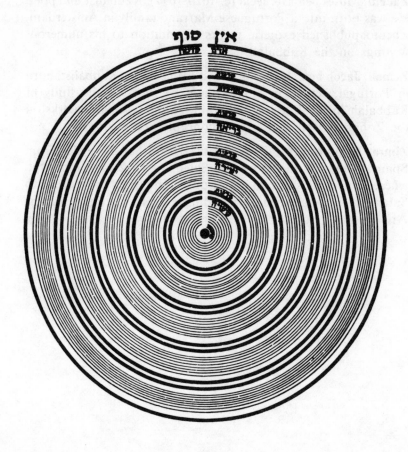

This chart designates that myriads of encircling Sephiroth, like layers of an onion, were gradually revealed in the vacuum, the principle point, Kingdom of the Infinite. The line of light which is issued from the Infinite is breaking through the roofs of all the circles. In general, they are subdivided into five worlds. These are:

1) The world of Adam Kadmon, Crown, from which man's soul derives its top degree of "Yechida."

2) World of Emanation, Wisdom. Man receives from it his spiritual essence of "Chayah."

3) World of Creation, Intelligence from which he gets his "Neshama."

4) World of Formation, Beauty from which "Ruach" is issued to man.

5) World of Action—our world, is the very middle point of the vacuum of Kingdom of the Infinite, Malchut. From this world "Nefesh" is extended to man.

Since Kingdom of the Infinite is the origin to all the worlds, therefore all the circles are connoted by the name of Kingdom, although, the upper circle in relation to its subsequent degrees is called Keter or Crown. Nevertheless, in relation to its origin it is but Kingdom, for Kingdom's last Sephira becomes the Crown to the first world, Adam Kadmon. In other words, the last degree of Kingdom of the Infinite is Kingdom, but in relation to Adam Kadmon it is Crown. The point in the centre is the last Sephira, Kingdom of the world of Action. It is the principal point of the six days, the Sabbath. It is also the heart of man. This is the meaning that every Israelite has a spark of God. It is the spark that he is demanded to sanctify, for its origin stems from the very source of all the sources, the Infinite world. We say it in our Sabbath prayer: "Come let us go to meet the Sabbath, for it is a wellspring of blessing; from the beginning, from of old it was ordained, last in production, first in thought."

APPENDIX II

The Sefirot — Relationship to man

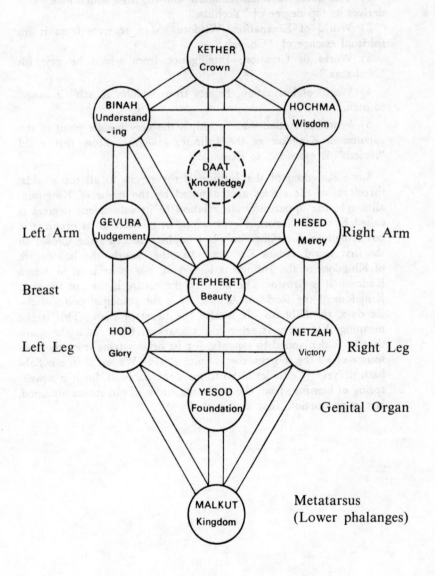

The body tree of man implies the interaction and two-way flow of the various parts of the human body. The complex clearing house is the skull, which assigns messages and cordinates ordinary consciousness.

APPENDIX III
The Sefirot
and

The Twelve Tribes, Months and Astrological Signs

We have learnt that Biblical narrative is the outer covering for many inner levels of concealed truths. An example of this is the story of Jacob and his twelve sons, who became the leaders of the twelve tribes of Israel. The chariot of the bottled-up energy (sefira) of Tiferet contains six sefirot-Hesed, Gevurah, Tiferet, Netzah, Hod, Yesod. Each of these sefirot in its male and female aspect can be attributed to one of the twelve sons, to the twelve months of the year, and to their astrological signs. Of the remaining four sefirot (Keter, Hokhmah, Binah, Malkhut), the upper three have no direct influence on this mundane level of existence, while Malkhut represents the Desire to Receive — Man himself, who is the ultimate recipient of all these energies.

The list below, which is derived from the words of Torah concerning the blessing given by Jacob to his sons, is presented for the reader's interest and information. A more detailed discussion of the subject will be found in a future volume on Astrology and the Kabbalah.

Sefira	Tribe	Months
Hesed	Reuben	Nissan
Gevurah	Shimon	Iyar
Tiferet	Levi	Sivan
Netzah	Yehuda	Tamuz
Hod	Yisechar	Av
Yesod	Zebulun	Elul
Hesed	Binyamin	Tishrei
Gevurah	Dan	Marhesvon
Tiferet	Naftali	Kislev
Netzah	Gad	Tevet
Hod	Asher	Shevat
Yesod	Yosef	Adar

Sign	English	Solar Equivalent
Taleh	Lamb	Aries
Shor	Ox	Taurus
Ti'umin	Twins	Gemini
Sartan	Crab	Cancer
Aryeh	Lion	Leo
Betulah	Virgin	Virgo
Ma'oznaim	Scales	Libra
Akrav	Scorpion	Scorpio
Keshet	Rainbow	Sagittarius
G'di	Goat	Capricorn
D'li	Vessel	Aquarius
Dagim	Fish	Pisces

APPENDIX IV
The Magen David

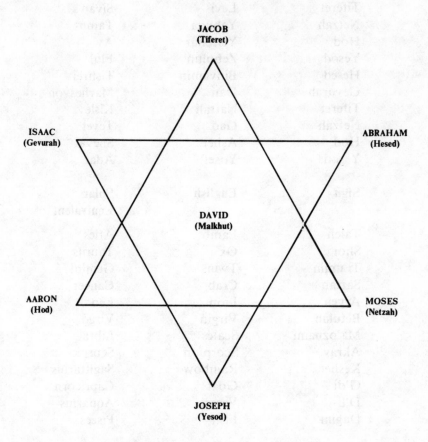

JACOB
(Tiferet)

ISAAC
(Gevurah)

ABRAHAM
(Hesed)

DAVID
(Malkhut)

AARON
(Hod)

MOSES
(Netzah)

JOSEPH
(Yesod)

The Shield of David, in a broader sense, implies the concept of cosmic consciousness. When a thorough knowledge of the Upper and Lower Triads has been achieved, then one can reach a Devekut with the cosmos which is represented by the Shield of David. Cosmic influences, namely the seven basic planets together with the twelve signs of the Zodiac are directly related and bound up with the above seven Sefirot. Each Sefirah is considered the internal energy of the seven planets which are as follows: Saturn, Jupiter, Mars, Sun, Venus, Mercury and the Moon in this order. Each planet rules over and dominates two signs of the Zodiac. The sun and moon rule over but one sign. Through Kabbalistic Meditation, one can connect with cosmic consciousness thereby achieving a level of pure awareness. When the individual has mastered the art of direct communion with and an attachment to the interiority of these cosmic influences, the Sefirot, then it is the individual who can now *direct* his destiny.

REFERENCES

Introduction

1. Zohar III, p. 183b, p. 297a.
2. Entrance to the Zohar, pp. 78-79, Jerusalem 1974, P.S. Berg, Research Centre of Kabbalah.
3. Zohar III, p. 58a, p. 85b. cf. Tractate Pesachim, 119a, Talmud Bavli, Talmud Eser Sefirot, Y. Ashlag, Vol. 1, p. 16, Tel Aviv 1957.
4. Zohar II, p. 7b.

Origins and History

5. Ethics of the Fathers, ch. I:1.
6. Tractate Tamid, p. 32a, Talmud Bavli.
7. Tractate Berakhot, 20a, Talmud Bavli.
8. Tikune Zohar, p. 1a, Zohar Hadash, p. 59.
9. Likutai Torah, p. 126, Vol. 12, 1970 Jerusalem, Research Centre of Kabbalah.
10. Gate of Reincarnation, p. 113, Vol. 13, 1970 Jerusalem, Research Centre of Kabbalah.
11. Zohar III, p. 100b.
12. Gate of the Parables of Rashbi, Vol. 6, p. 91, Tel Aviv, 1969, Research Centre of Kabbalah.

Rabbi Shimon Bar Yohai and the Greater Assembly

13. Zohar I, p. 11a.
14. Rabbis Abba, Yehuda, Yosi ben Jacob, Yitzhak, Hezekiah ben Rav, Chiya, Yosi and Yisa.
15. Zohar III, Idra Rabba, p. 127b.
16. Zohar III, Idra Rabba, p. 144a.
17. Zohar III, Idra Rabba p. 144a.
18. Zohar Hadash, Vayyera p. 26b.
19. Zohar I, p. 24a, cf. Ashlag ed.

20. Zohar I. p. 174b.
21. Zohar III, Deuteronomy, p. 287b.

The Golden Age of Safed

22. Isaiah, ch. 2:3.
23. Exodus, ch. 34:23.
24. Exodus, ch. 21:2.
25. Gate of Reincarnation, p. 133, Jerusalem 1978, Research Centre.
26. Gate of Reincarnation, p. 129, Jerusalem 1978, Research Centre.
27. Gate of Reincarnation, p. 135, Jerusalem, 1978 Research Centre.
28. Ibid. p. 135.
29. Ibid. p. 136.
30. Ibid. p. 136.
31. Ibid. p. 138.
32. Ibid. p. 138.
33. Ibid. p. 156.
34. Ibid. p. 156.
35. Ibid. p. 139.
36. Ibid. p. 148.

A Later Light — Rabbi Ashlag

37. For full text, see Entrance to the Zohar, Philip S. Berg, Jerusalem 1974, p. 7, Research Centre of Kabbalah.
38. Zohar II, p. 7b.
39. Zohar III, p. 23a.
40. Zohar III, p. 58a.
41. Tractate Berakhot, p. 20a.

The Body of Knowledge

42. Autobiography p. 127.

43. Deut, ch. 12:23.
44. Zohar III, p. 152a.
45. Zohar III, p. 99b.

Main Teachings

46. Etz Haim, Gate I, Branch II. cf. Ten Luminous Emanations, Vol. 1, p. 33, Jerusalem 1972, Research Centre of
Kabbalah.
47. Talmud Eser Sefirot, Vol. 1, p. 6, Hebrew 1956, Research
Centre. This same idea is expressed on p. 72, of the Ten
Luminous Emanations, Vol. 1.
48. Ibid. p. 67.
49. Ibid. p. 67.

Major Concepts

50. Zohar I, p. 164a.
51. Sefer Hakdamot, p. 52, Research Centre 1978.
52. Zohar I, 15b.
53. Isaiah, ch. 6:3.
54. Ten Luminous Emanations, Vol. 1, p. 64, Research Centre
1978.
55. Genesis, ch. 1:1-8.
56. Genesis, ch. 25:5,6.
57. Zohar I, p. 133b. cf. Zohar I, p. 223a.
58. Zohar I, p. 133b.
59. Ibid. p. 133b.
60. Exodus, ch. 19:3.
61. Judges, ch. 5:4.
62. Zohar III, p. 192a.
63. Zohar III, p. 192b.
64. Zohar III, p. 192b.
65. Zohar III, p. 193a.
66. Exodus, ch. 19:4.

67. Genesis ch. 18.1.
68. Genesis ch. 25:28.
69. Ibid. ch. 25:27.
70. Ibid. ch. 32:29.
71. Exodus, ch. 17:11.
72. Midrash Rabba, Chukkas.
73. Tractate M'Nahoth, p. 29b, Talmud Bavli, cf. Gates of Reincarnation, p. 103, Jerusalem 1978, Research Centre.
74. Midrash Rabbah, Vayhi.
75. Tractate M'Nahoth, p. 29b, Talmud Bavli.
76. Deut., ch. 4:4.
77. Zohar III, Idra Rabba, p. 143a.
78. Gate of Reincarnation, p. 79, Vol. 13, Jerusalem, Research Centre.
79. Exodus, ch. 2:2.
80. Gate of Reincarnation, p. 97, Vol. 13, 1978 Jerusalem, Research Centre.
81. Tractate Pesachim, p. 49b, Talmud Bavli.
82. Zohar III, p. 151b.
83. Genesis, ch. 41.56. cf. Zohar I, p. 197a.
84. Zohar Hadash, p. 67c.
85. Ten Luminous Emanations, Vol. 1, p. 55-76, Jerusalem 1978, Research Centre.
86. Ibid. p. 74.
87. Zohar I, p. 34a.
88. Zohar I, p. 18a.
89. Ten Luminous Emanations, Vol. 1, p. 76, Jerusalem 1978, Research Centre.
90. Zohar II, p. 176a.
91. Malahai ch. 3:6.
92. Zohar I, p. 15a.

Practical Applications — Operational Tools

93. Tractate Shabbat, p. 31a.

94. Genesis, ch. 8:21.
95. Ibid. ch. 22:1-19.
96. Ibid. ch. 22:1.
97. Zohar I, p. 119a.
98. Genesis, ch. 22:10-12.
99. Exodus, ch. 34:26.
100. Zohar 11, p. 125a.
101. Leviticus, ch. 18.19.
102. Zohar III, p. 79a.
103. Rabbi Isaac Luria, Sefer Lekutai Torah V'Taamai ha-Mitzvot, p. 34. Jerusalem 1970, Research Centre.
104. Tractate Kiddushim, p. 2a.
105. Ibid. p. 7a.
106. Ibid. p. 5b.
107. Chronicles I, ch. 28:9.
108. Genesis, ch. 4:1.
109. Rabbi Isaac Luria, Sefer Sh'ar ha-Kavvonot, p. 2, Tel Aviv 1962.
110. Zohar III, p. 218b.
111. Zohar I, p. 50b.

GLOSSARY OF KABBALISTIC TERMINOLOGY

Akedat Yitzhak — The Binding of Isaac — The containing of the negative energy, left column, of the sefira of Gevurah (Isaac), in order to bring about harmony with the positive, right column energy of the sefira of Hesed (Avraham).

Arousal — Awakening in the vessel of desire to impart and receive.

Bar/Bat Mitzvah — The time at which the aspect of imparting in the soul awakens, age thirteen in the male and twelve in the female.

Bread of Shame — Shame at receiving that which is not earned.

Cables — Various means for the transference of positive metaphysical energies to man (such as, prayer, meditation, Shabbat, the Festivals, etc.).

Central Column — Synthesizer and synthesis of the left and right (negative and positive energies).

Circular Concept — The balance between left and right, negative and positive, brought about by use of restriction. Central column.

Correction — The task of bringing the universe to a state of perfection. (Tikun).

Creator — The source of all positive energy.

Desire to Receive — Negativity. The aspect of drawing or taking. In our universe all is made up of the "Desire to Receive". On the physical level, a "desire to receive for itself alone", characterized by selfishness, egotism, materialism in man must be transmuted to a "desire to receive in order to impart" — a balance and harmony between receiving and imparting permitting the individual to draw into himself the positive light of the Creator.

Desire to Impart — Positivity. The aspect of giving characteristic of the Creator (See above: Creator, Desire to Receive).

Devekut — Cleaving. Fulfillment of circular concept whereby union is brought about between the light of G-d, and man.

Din — Judgment. Energy drawn by the left column without the use of the right and central columns, causing a metaphysical imbalance, spiritual disharmony in the individual.

En-Sof — Endless World, World of the Infinite, The first world from which sprang all future emanations. The primal world in which the souls of man were in perfect harmony with the Creator. A complete balance between the endless imparting of the Creator and the endless receiving of his creations — the souls of man.

Gematria — System of numerology used for Biblical interpretation and mystical enlightenment of the more hidden aspects of Torah

Gemarrah — See "Talmud".

G-d — Source of all positivity.

G'mar Ha-Tikun — The final redemption of Israel — ultimate peace by harmony in the world. (See Correction.)

G'vurah — Power, Might. The second of the seven sefirot. Left column — Chariot of Isaac.

Halakha — Code of Jewish Law. The system through which the Jew can attune himself to the true flow of spiritual energies of G-d (Ha-Shem).

Hassidism — A movement founded by the Ba'al Shem Tov on kabbalistic principles. The key to all of life and worship of G-d is through joy and happiness.

Haiya — Fourth level of soul of man.

Hesed — Mercy — First of the seven sefirot — Right column — Chariot of Avraham.

Hod — Splendor — Fifth of the seven sefirot — Left Column Chariot of Aaron.

Idra Rabba — The greater Assembly. The meeting of Rabbi Shimon bar Yohai, his son, Rabbi Elazar, and eight disciples. The first instance in history of a group of people learning Kabbalah. From this group came the Sefer Ha-Zohar.

Idra Zuta — The lesser assembly — Day of death of R. Shimon bar Yohai.

Kashrut — Dietary laws to keep the Jew in metaphysical and spiritual harmony.

Klippot — Shells, evil husks created by man's negative deeds which "cover" and limit man in his spiritual development. The barriers between man and the light of G-d.

Lag B'Omer — Day of the death of R. Shimon bar Yohai. Thirty-third day of Sefirot Ha-Omer. This day coincides with the cessation of the plague that killed 24,000 disciples of R. Akiva. Hod shebe'Hod of the forty-nine sefirot between Pesach and Shavuot. (See Sifirot Ha-Omer.)

Left Column — The column (channel) through which are drawn all metaphysical energies. (See Desire to Receive.)

Lower Vessels — the vessels having the larger Desire to Receive.

Malakh — Supernal Angel or energy force devoid of any physical manifestation of a desire to receive.

Malkhut — Kingdom — The tenth and final sefira from Keter. The sefira in which the greatest desire to receive is manifest and in which all correction takes place. The physical world.

Merkhvah — Chariots (Abraham, Isaac, Jacob, etc.) with the metaphysical ability to combine metaphysical forces with mundane, physical entities.

Messiah/The Age of the Messiah — The end of the period of correction and the beginning of an era of universal peace and harmony. The Messiah is the symbol by which man is shown that the "Correction" has been completed and is not, as in the common misconception, the *means* to the correction itself.

Midrash Rabba — Collection of interpretations, poetic reflections and homilies on the Torah and the Five Scrolls.

Middle Point — Name of the fourth phase of the En-Sof. Called the middle point because of its absolute unity with the infinite light of G-d (Ha-Shem).

Mikvah — A body of water through which the individual enclothed in *Din* is brought into spiritual balance. More specifically for women after the period of *Niddah.* Also used by men to remove Klippot and thereby further their spiritual development. *Maim Haim,* "living water", such as springs, rivers, etc. The water of the Mikvah is an extremely powerful channel for positive energies.

Mishna — Oral teachings of Judaism — the collection of writings of the Tannaim on all aspects of Judaism.

Nefesh — Lowest of the five levels of the soul. Correlated with the Sefira of Malkhut.

Neshama — Third of the five levels of the soul. Correlated with the sefira of Binah.

Netzah — Victory — Fourth of the seven sefirot. Chariot of Moses.

Niddah — The period of menstruation plus seven clean days after. During this time the female is over-charged with the energies of the left column with no corresponding arousal for the right column. A time of metaphysical disturbance in the female neutralized only by immersion in a Mikveh seven days after cessation of menstruation.

Nigleh — Revealed — specifically the revealed aspect of the Torah, Talmud, Halakha, etc.

Nistar — The concealed, hidden wisdom of the Torah.

Olam En-Sof — See En-Sof.

Olamot — Frameworks of reference used in the study of Kabbalah; usually connected with various degrees of the "Desire to Receive".

Or-Light — The supreme emanation of the Creator.

Or Ein Sof — Light of the Infinite, endless.

Or Makif — Encircling Light. The spiritual light surrounding every individual. It is the task of each person to draw this encircling light into himself and thus spiritually elevate himself.

Or Pnimi — Inner Light. The inner energy of a human being that maintains him physically. The energy responsible for all physical growth.

Partzuf — Complete structure

Right Column — Column that draws the energy of imparting — the positive force. The aspect of the "Desire to Impart".

Sefirot — The vessels through which the light of the Creator is emanated to man.

Sefer Yitzira — The Book of Formation. First known kabbalistic work containing in concise, highly esoteric language, the entire teachings of Kabbalah. Attributed to either Avraham or Rabbi Akiva.

Shabbat — The final day of each week (Saturday) in which the Jew is enclothed solely in positivity.

Similarity of Form — When the Desire to Receive is in balance with the Desire to Impart, there is then a situation whereby the individual is receiving for the sake of imparting. Therefore, a "similiarity of form" comes about with the imparting of the individual being similar to the imparting of the Creator, and thus a union can take place between the individual and the light of G-d.

Sitrei-Torah — The deepest hidden teachings of the Torah received only through divine revelation.

Sod — Secret, inner meaning.

Ta'amei Torah — The reasons of Torah — The teaching through which one reaches the true inner meanings of Torah and thereby elevates oneself to the highest degrees of spirituality.

Talmud — The written form of the oral law. The main work of Judaic studies. A compilation of Mishna, Tosfot, Gemorrah.

Talmud Eser Ha'Sefirot — A study of the emanations of the Sefirot, vital for any deep understanding of the workings of our universe. Written by R. Yehuda Ashlag.

Tannaim — Teachers of Jewish law in the 1st to 3rd centuries. Their teachings are known as the Mishna.

Tefillin — Phylacteries — small black boxes containing certain Torah portions. Tefillin are placed on the left arm and head. The Tefillin of the arm is to bind and contain the left column energy of the desire to receive for itself alone — to turn this to a desire to receive in order to impart — a balance of left in harmony with right. The Tefillin of the head is to connect with the positive energy and subsequent cosmic consciousness and pure awareness.

Tikunei Ha-Zohar — Separate section of the Sefer ha-Zohar by R. Shimon bar Yohai, not contained in the main body of the Zohar itself. Its teachings are specifically geared to the Age of the Messiah.

Torah — In its broader sense, the entire doctrine of Judaism, written and oral, including all commentaries, past and future. In its restricted sense it refers to the Pentateuch, the five books of Moses.

Tosfat Shabbat — The extra soul one receives on Shabbat in order to enable him to reach a higher state of spiritual consciousness. Through the "Tosfat Shabbat" the Jew's vessel for receiving is vastly enlarged enabling him to draw forth more positive energies than would normally be possible.

Tumah — Unclean,impure. A state of total metaphysical imbalance. When there is a manifestation of the Desire to Receive for itself alone, the resulting imbalance is the energy of "Tumah".

Tsimtsum — The voluntary rejection or restriction of the Divine Light in the Olam En Sof due to the aspect of bread of Shame and the desire to identify with the aspect of sharing and imparting. In the lower worlds this restriction is no longer voluntary but imposed and constitutes one of the basic rules by which our mundane world must operate.

Veils — Metaphysical barriers brought about by our own negative actions. The veils refuse entry to the light of the Creator and completely limit the individual's spiritual potential.

Vessel — Containers of the Divine Light derived from the Desire to Receive and growing in thickness from level to level until they are co-terminous with the world of the senses where the light is practically invisible. Also referred to as bottled — up energies.

Yehida — Highest level of soul. Total oneness — union with the light of G-d. A level unobtainable until the coming of the Messiah. Correlated with the Sefira of Keter.

Yesh Me-Ayin — Something from Nothing. See Appendix — Creation.

Yesod — Sixth of the seven Sefirot. The Sefira through which is emanated all light to our world. Chariot of Yosef.

Yetzer ha-Rah — Mans evil inclination- The desire to receive for itself alone.

INDEX

Impart 85
— nature of light 78, 85
Imparting 73, 76, 128
— positive force 70
Inanimate 20, 71, 72
Incarnation 38, 40, 42, 123
Infinite 77, 89, 164
Inner Light 24, 28, 105
Intelligence 102
Internal Energy 112, 172
Isaac 96, 97, 103
— Akeda 99, 123-126, 172
Isaac ben Todros 153
Isaac the Blind 153
Isabella, Queen 31
Isaiah, Prophet 32, 36, 88
Ishmael 98
Ishmael, R 153
Israel 32, 47, 65, 80, 98, 100, 104, 123, 136, 141
Israel, Baal Shem 139, 140, 154
Iyar 170

J

Jacob 94, 103, 128, 172
Jacob ben Jacob 154
Jerusalem 32, 34, 36
Jewish Esotericism 107
Johanan ben Zakai 104, 150
Joseph
— as Chariot 106, 172
Joseph Ibn Shraga 154
Joseph Ibn Tabul 155
Judah ben Kalonymus 155

Judah ben Samuel 155
Judaism 11, 12, 14, 15, 47, 99, 105, 139, 141
Judgment 96, 103, 107, 130
Jupiter 172

K

Kabbalistic Meditation 161, 172
Kabbalistic Astrology 170
Kalba Shevua 41, 148
Karo 23, 40, 148, 155
Kashrut 129, 180
Kavannah 141
Keshet 170
Keter 102, 107
Kiddush 64
Kingdom of En Sof 89, 115
Kislev 170
Klippot 39, 180, 181
Knowledge 64, 137
Korah 38

L

Lag B'omer 30, 180
Lamb 170
Language
— restriction of 52, 58, 60, 65
Law, Jewish 32, 33, 37, 65, 98, 102
Lecha Dodi 33, 148
Left Column 102, 103, 105, 106, 128, 143, 144, 180
— Gevurah 103, 105
Leo 170